The Insider's Guide to Egg Donation

A Compassionate and Comprehensive Guide for All Parents-to-Be

DATE DUE

Demco, Inc. 38-293

The Insider's Guide to Egg Donation

A Compassionate and Comprehensive Guide for All Parents-to-Be

By
Wendie Wilson-Miller
and
Erika Napoletano

demosHEALTH
NEW YORK

ISBN: 978-1-936303-30-4
E-ISBN: 978-1-617051-04-3

Acquisitions Editor: Noreen Henson
Cover Design: Carlos Maldonado
Compositor: Absolute Service, Inc.

Visit our Web site at www.demosmedpub.com

Medical information provided by Demos Health, in the absence of a visit with a healthcare professional, must be considered as an educational service only. This book is not designed to replace a physician's independent judgment about the appropriateness or risks of a procedure or therapy for a given patient. Our purpose is to provide you with information that will help you make your own healthcare decisions.

The information and opinions provided here are believed to be accurate and sound, based on the best judgment available to the authors, editors, and publisher, but readers who fail to consult appropriate health authorities assume the risk of any injuries. The publisher is not responsible for errors or omissions. The editors and publisher welcome any reader to report to the publisher any discrepancies or inaccuracies noticed.

CIP data is available from the Library of Congress

Special discounts on bulk quantities of Demos Health books are available to corporations, professional associations, pharmaceutical companies, healthcare organizations, and other qualifying groups. For details, please contact:

Special Sales Department
Demos Medical Publishing
11 W. 42nd Street
New York, NY 10036
Phone: 800-532-8663 or 212-683-0072
Fax: 212-941-7842
E-mail: rsantana@demosmedpub.com

Printed in the United States of America by Hamilton Printing.
12 13 14 15   5 4 3 2 1

Dedicated to every person on the journey toward family.

I'd like to thank the first family I donated to for helping me realize
my passion in life, and the others for allowing me to be a part of
something special beyond words.
To my husband for his extraordinary patience with me
through all of my projects.
To Tina, my best friend, confidant, and the person who keeps me
laughing through it all.
To my co-author Erika and our agent Stephany Evans, without
whom this book would not have been possible.
And last, but not least, to my parents whose continued generosity
and faith in me allow my dreams to come true.

-Wendie

A simple thank you to all of the families who trusted me with helping
them achieve their dreams.
To our agent, Stephany Evans, for her tireless work on this
book's road to publication.
And to my parents for some great genes.

-Erika

Contents

Contents

Foreword

Like any how-to book, the quality of this book is defined by the quality of the writing and the qualifications of the authors. Unlike my experience, which has been spread across all areas of reproductive endocrinology and infertility, Wendie and Erika can share their experiences from the nonmedical side of the donor process. They're the ones, day in and day out, working to help families like yours achieve your dreams. Although they will each share their own stories about how they came to be egg donors—and in Wendie's case, an agency owner—I can tell you from a medical perspective that there has never been a guide available like the one they've put together for you. With a perfect combination of expertise, experience, and compassion, these women have achieved a book that is eminently readable, entertaining, and fully informative. This book is certain to become the standard text for anyone facing fertility challenges, who is seeking information on egg donation.

My personal journey through infertility from medical student to fertility specialist to even being a fertility patient myself has been both joyous and harrowing. What I have come to realize is that the joy of this journey comes from the journey itself and the amazing people like Wendie and Erika with whom I have shared it. I have no doubt you'll find that what follows will be instrumental in your journey toward family and will help open your arms to the women all over the world who have become egg donors. Although you may choose to never meet your donor, I can share this with you: they're in your corner and want nothing more than to hear they've helped you achieve your dream.

Read on and rest assured that what's to follow will answer your questions and put you at ease. If these two ladies (and all of the experts who have contributed) could, they'd be right there beside you to hold your hand as you walk toward the family of your dreams.

Daniel A. Potter, MD, FACOG
Laguna Beach, California

Preface

We are not doctors or nurses. We aren't trained psychological professionals. Only one of us is a parent.

Then why are we writing a book for people trying to start families?

We're women. For all you know, we could be your next-door neighbors or the gals behind you in line at the grocery store. But we're women with a unique perspective that helps us understand what you're dealing with and how many times you felt like banging your head (or someone else's, for that matter) into a wall throughout the frustrating journey down the road of the fertility challenged.

We know a thing or two about egg donation, and over the past eleven years, we've picked up a story or two to share. Maybe they'll inspire you as they have us.

Wendie: Egg Donor Agency Owner, Twelve-Year Industry Veteran, and Multiple Cycle Egg Donor

The night before the retrieval procedure, I met Anna (name has been changed) and her husband. Anna needed an egg donor because she was in remission from cancer and a donor was her only hope to conceive a child. We'd never met prior to this though we'd been synced up. We all went out to dinner, and over the next few hours we laughed, cried, and talked. This one dinner changed my life. My decision to become an egg donor brought tears to a couple's eyes, hopes to their hearts, and told me that there was more to my decision than I'd ever considered. I had to find a way to make this—egg donation—a part of my life.

I had been reading about egg donation since college. When I moved to Southern California, I started hearing about it again. It was interesting enough to me to pick up the phone and call the egg donor agency where my journey began. I filled out an application and went through their screening process. It wasn't long before I was matched with Anna. Meeting with her was enough for me to know that I wanted to be involved in the process beyond being just a donor.

I spoke to the agency owner about being more involved and discovered the agency was one of the most prominent egg donor agencies in the country. Over the next year I worked as a marketing assistant for the agency part time and soon took a position as a junior cycle coordinator for the donor program. I loved what I did each and every day: helping people build families. Although there was still the occasional donor cycle here and there, my real passion was in helping recipients learn about the egg donation process, match them with donors, and work with the donors and IVF clinics to make cycles as successful as possible.

Within the next few years I became the supervising director of the entire egg donor program and continued with that agency for eight and a half years before starting my own firm. During that time, I coordinated somewhere in the neighborhood of 1,000 donor cycles that resulted in the most wonderful things: happy parents, delighted donors, and notes of thanks. This is a joy-filled business!

It's also a people business. Although this may sound trite, it is true on so many levels. As a reproductive industry professional, I build relationships with everyone from psychologists to pharmacists to doctors and travel agencies. My job is to take care of everyone involved in making babies—and families—a reality. I'm extremely fortunate to have developed long-term friendships with some of the industry's leading voices and practitioners. What many don't consider is that working in this industry is about real world experience. I was asked to join the board of Parents Via Egg Donation (*http://www.pved.com*), the leading educational resource for the egg donation industry, in 2009, and am delighted to be a part of shaping the future of egg donation.

Every cycle has its nuances. Each recipient is different. Every donor is beautiful. There's a certain satisfaction that I get from knowing that no matter how different the people we work with are, we help guide them toward that universal goal: family.

Erika: Multiple Cycle Egg Donor Whose Recipients Have Over 15 Children Between Them

It was a summer day in 2008 when I saw her. Golden pageboy hair blowing from her face with each whoosh of the swing and a cherubic face that reminded me of those square pictures held down by black corners in my parents' vinyl-covered, ring-bound photo albums.

Pictures of me.

I looked over at her dad. He was smiling. I looked at Wendie. She was smiling. Then Wendie asked me, "So, how do you feel?"

"It's cool. Very, very cool," I said. Because it was.

I first met Alysson (name has been changed) when she was just over a year old. We—her parents, Wendie, and me—got together at a Studio City cafe so

I could meet her. You see, there's a part of me that helped her parents' dreams come true. Her parents had their first daughter and while trying for their second child, they learned that Barbara (name has been changed) was going through early menopause in her late 30s. If they were going to have another child, they were going to need an egg donor. And that's how they met me.

Back in 2000, I'd just returned to the United States after living in Japan. I was a personal trainer at the time, and a colleague mentioned to me that she was going to see her boys that afternoon.

"I didn't know you had kids! How old are they?" I asked.

"Oh, they're not really 'my boys.' They're my best friend's twin sons and they're about eight months old," she replied. "I was her egg donor. I visit with them all the time!"

My eyes got wide. *Egg donor*—you can do that? Over the next few weeks, I plied her with questions, and she told me everything. I thought *this is incredibly cool*. What a wonderful gift. So I did my due diligence and connected with a well-respected egg donor agency in Los Angeles (which is how Wendie and I became friends). Five years later, I'd helped multiple families bring fifteen children into the world. There could be more—and some days, I wonder.

Over those five years, I'd virtually passed out from my first shot of stimulating hormones and hyperstimulated to the point that I appeared six months pregnant. Yet on the other side of the coin, I've met one of the children who is part me, staring with fascination as she swung on a playground swing while chatting with her dad. It's a humbling, selfless, and awe-inspiring journey, being an egg donor. But why did I do it?

Because all I could think is that I was sitting here with perfectly good eggs that people needed. And from the first note I received from a recipient couple, I knew I'd made the right decision.

AN INVITATION TO BEGIN

Now that you know a bit more about us and why we decided to write a book on egg donation, let's get you started. Regardless of why you've arrived at egg donation's doorstep, there's a wealth of information in the pages following to guide you on your journey toward family. To date, there are more than 51,000 children brightening families' lives because of egg donor technology. We would love to be a part of helping you become the next family that experiences this unparalleled joy.

Let's take a look inside the egg donor industry and all of its glorious pieces and get you the information you need about the incredible gift of modern medical technology waiting for you. And the one thing we promise? You'll hear what it's all about from the people who know it best: doctors, nurses, donors, and recipients. People just like you.

Acknowledgments

We can't express enough gratitude to the fertility industry professionals who shared their time and expertise with us during the course of the writing of this book. Although we developed the vision for what this book would ultimately be, it certainly wouldn't have been possible without them.

A special thanks to our families and friends as well, for putting up with us through numerous deadlines, late nights, early mornings, and everything else that came with putting this project together.

Contributing professionals are as follows, in no particular order but with equal affection: Lauri de Brito; Lilly Frost; Marna Gatlin; Abigail Glass; Stephanie Goldman-Levich; Brenda Hardt-Fahn; John Hesla; Kathryn Kaycoff-Manos; Bradford Kolb; Elliott Kronenfeld; Steven Lazarus; Kate Lyon; Daniel Potter; Guy Ringler; Gregory Rosen; Vicken Sahakian; Eric Scott Sills; David Tourgeman; Amy Vance; and Carole Lieber Wilkins.

Introduction: A Different Kind of Stork

Get over yourself. Like I said, it's do or die. Go in, balls to the wall and say, "I'm going to do this, I don't care how long it takes."
—Lynn McDonnell, mother, hardcase recipient parent

If you've landed here, it's not by accident. You're looking for answers, assistance, and more importantly, a family. And we're here to tell you you're not alone.

According to the Centers for Disease Control's (CDC) 2002 National Survey of Family Growth, 16.6% of those of childbearing age face infertility. That figure translates to one in every seven couples in the United Kingdom. The World Health Organization says 8%–10% of couples worldwide face it.

What this means (in terms your reproductive endocrinologist will never use):

- At the Gym: If your spin class has 21 people in it, two of them are just like you.

- In Professional Sports: Out of 53 rostered players on an NFL team, seven are just like you.

- In the Arts: Out of more than 100 members currently on the roster at the Gay Men's Chorus of Los Angeles, fourteen to sixteen are just like you.

- In the City: Houston, Texas has an estimated population of 2.2 million people as of 2008. That means that in Houston alone, there are 314,285 (maybe more) people just like you.

If you want to bring the numbers closer to home, insert your own city's population data and divide by seven.

But unlike those who only need a little help with their own genetic material, you're here because you're considering using a different kind of stork to deliver your bundle of joy: an egg donor.

Why Egg Donation?

Since egg donor technology appeared in the early 1980s, more than 51,000 children have joined families otherwise unable to conceive. If other means of assisted reproduction have failed you and you're considering egg donation, there's one thing of which we're certain:

> Those looking for an egg donor often want children more than those who were able to have them the old-fashioned way.

When you crave something, you change everything else in your life to have it. You work an extra job, you change your schedule, you sacrifice. You find a way to make it happen, regardless of the consequences. We understand that craving, and we don't take it lightly. We're here as a resource that you can trust to hand it to you straight, tell you now what's important, and let you know that every person and family exploring egg donation, although different as eggs themselves, share a certain path. Although you might never have expected to pick this book up, we'll make you glad that you did.

A Book for Every Type of Family

Infertility isn't just about eggs and sperm not playing nice in the sandbox. As you can see by our "arts" example earlier, there are inarguable biological barriers that some individuals and couples face on the road to family. If you're a traditional, heterosexual family, your journey is much different from what society considers nontraditional families. From single moms to same-sex and transgendered couples, society often has had difficulty seeing that the urge to parent extends beyond what is perceived as "normal."

What you all have in common is that you want a family, can't make one the old-fashioned way, and you need information beyond the chirpy optimist in your support group who says, "Ohhhh, you just have to be patient!" This is a guide for what to expect when you weren't expecting this. Egg donation is a beautiful gift of science that makes the dream of family accessible to you. We're here to help you understand and embrace the process. Because that other stuff; patience? We know. It's not working.

Although the traditional way of making a family is still working for some, alternative solutions are ever more available and are no longer "in the closet." Today, fertility challenges are fair game for conversation. Advertisements run in newspapers to recruit egg donors. Celebrities make headlines by adopting children. Same-sex couples and singles seek parenthood with increasing frequency. No matter your beliefs, we understand the desire to become parents is universal and when looking at the current resources available, we saw there was no definitive guide available that

- educated audiences about the egg donation process
- addressed all types of families
- offered a road map for those embarking on the journey toward a family through egg donation

This is where we come in. Although we can't tell you that your own journey through egg donation won't have its own unique footprint, we can tell you that we're the best ones to fill you in on the best practices, what to expect, and how to make the process your own.

1

Egg Donation—The Basics

Let's step back to 1977 and take a peek into the life of Leslie Brown. After struggling with infertility for more than nine years because of a tubal factor, she never thought her struggles would make her a household name in the world of fertility. In July of 1978, Leslie gave birth to her daughter, the aptly named Louise Joy Brown, the first child born as a result of an in vitro fertilization (IVF) procedure.

No matter how long you've faced fertility challenges, we're sure each of you can imagine what it felt like for Leslie to hold dear Louise in her arms. Whatever fears she had about IVF and all of the heartache she faced through those nine years was instantly trumped by a beautiful little girl's smile. A gift of modern medicine and reproductive technology, little Louise paved the way for the path you're on right now.

Because both of us have not only been egg donors but also worked (and in Wendie's case, still works daily) with recipient parents, we understand the myriad of questions that already have—and eventually will—roll through your mind. Although the egg donation process has many facets from both the recipient and donor side, we've built this book to give you a step-by-step approach to understanding what you need to know and when. Although it might seem small, it is now estimated that approximately 1% of all births[1] in the United States are the result of assisted reproductive technology (ART). That's the 1% you want to join. Let's begin the journey by looking at why egg donation has become a reality in today's medical landscape and how your own scenario weaves into the path toward building a family using this incredible technology.

THE HISTORY OF EGG DONATION

Although Leslie Brown and her daughter offered new hope for fertility-challenged families as far back as 1978, egg donation didn't emerge as a

1

realistic option until 1983. That year, the first pregnancy from an egg donation procedure was reported in the United States, and the world of reproductive medicine was, once again, forever changed. Women's dreams of motherhood were no longer limited by their own genetic material. Today we see families of all shapes, sizes, and makeups looking toward donor egg technology to build homes and futures with children of their own.

THE BASICS OF ASSISTED REPRODUCTION USING DONOR EGGS

If you've already read this far, it's pretty unlikely that you're unfamiliar with the moving parts of an assisted reproduction cycle. No matter if you're male or female, we'll simply outline all of the components that come together to make a donor egg cycle a reality.

- **The intended parent(s):** For whatever reason, your situation requires that you need donor eggs to build your family. This can be as simple as single males, gay, or transgendered couples who lack genetic material to female factors such as early onset of menopause, previous cancer treatments, or other various factors inhibiting egg viability.

- **Your reproductive endocrinologist:** These are medical professionals who have dedicated their careers to technologies that help the fertility challenged achieve parenthood. More than just OB/GYNs, they're traditionally board certified in this very specific field of health by the American Board of Obstetrics and Gynecology.

- **Your egg donor:** These are women who typically register with various third-party egg donor agencies or internal donor programs at reproductive clinics. The ideal age for donors per the American Society for Reproductive Medicine (ASRM) guidelines is between 21 and 34, with the higher age ranges being reserved for proven donors. They represent every possible cultural, religious, and lifestyle background (just like the families for whom they donate) and are compensated for their time and effort during the donor cycle. Most egg donations performed worldwide are anonymous, meaning that the donor and intended parent(s) never meet. However, this trend is shifting toward more known donations than the industry's ever seen before.

Because we will go into much further detail about the egg donor cycle and the other key people you might find a part of your cycle in Chapter 7, we'll outline the basics to get you going. Whether cycling with the intended mother or with a surrogate, the menstrual cycles of both the donor and female who will eventually receive the embryo transfer are synced through the use of birth control pills and certain suppression hormones. The donor then receives a series of stimulating hormones to mature as many eggs as possible prior to retrieval to increase the chances of multiple viable embryos once fertilized. For the carrying female, she receives estrogen and progesterone to prepare the uterine lining for the transferred embryos. Finally, the donor undergoes the egg retrieval process, and the eggs are then sent for IVF with the intended father's or donor sperm. After fertilization and a certain time frame, the intended mother or surrogate will then undergo embryo transfer and await a pregnancy result.

All of the procedures directly related to your egg donor cycle are outpatient surgeries, and with our guidance, our hope is that you'll be surrounded on your journey by a collection of friendly, experienced professionals dedicated to helping fulfill your dreams.

EGG DONATION BY THE NUMBERS

We began this book in a way we hoped would help you understand that you're not alone in facing fertility challenges. In fact, the Centers for Disease Control and Prevention report more than 148,000 ART cycles performed in the United States during 2008.[2] In the United Kingdom, that number settles in at roughly 54,000.[3] But beyond that, those looking to egg donation have a very specific set of statistics to help guide your decisions.

In 2008, there were 18,121 ART cycles performed using donor eggs (12% of all ART cycles performed that year).[4] That was an increase of 40% over the figures reported in 2006 where only 10,984 donor egg cycles were reported. In 2006 and 2008, respectively, these donor cycles resulted in 54% and 55% live birth success rates. In the United Kingdom, 2006 figures were 1,278 cycles with a 30% live birth rate,[5] and 2008 figures were 1,700 cycles with a 28.5% live birth rate.[6]

Each year, the number of people who look to egg donors to build the family of their dreams is increasing, and right alongside those increases are the ever-improving technologies. If you think back from 1977 when no children joined families on account of reproductive technology to today where in the United States, more than 50% of all egg donor cycles bring children into our world, that's a beautiful set of statistics to guide your journey. Your reproductive specialist can offer you additional statistics specific to your personal scenario, but from our perspective, we can offer this: Statistics offers a solid foundation for helping guide your decision-making process, but never forget that in the case of family, your heart must also be a guide. That's part of the reason we're both egg donors (because that's a decision that is pretty much all heart) and why Wendie has moved forward with her career to found her own egg donor agency. The science, although never exact, takes care of itself while we get to help people work through the heart of a very personal matter.

How Egg Donor Agencies Help Your Journey—One Intended Mother's Thoughts

"I would say to anyone out there, and to me, this was the most critical part of the process—the agency is KEY. Their philosophy is going to translate to the young women they recruit. If you have an agency that is superficial and churning out donors like they are exotic cars, that is the type of donor they are going to attract. If you have an agency with lovely people who are compassionate to your struggle and believe that they are going to match you with a wonderful donor, then that is what you are going to get. Our agency was an instrumental part of getting the egg donor experience we wanted."—*Anonymous Intended Mother*

INTRODUCING THE EGG DONOR AGENCY

A mere six years following that first successful pregnancy via an egg donation procedure in 1983, the first egg donation cycle coordinated via a third-party agency became a reality. We'll go into detail in Chapter 5 on the practicalities of evaluating and eventually choosing an egg donor agency. But for now, let's talk about agencies that can help you on this journey.

Your egg donor agency's role is to not only be your partner but also your logistics coordinator, due diligence manager, counselor, confidant, and companion as you proceed with egg donation. Whereas agencies range in experience, reputation, relationships, and other factors, the one you ultimately choose can lend you insight and skills that will not only ease the process but also help you focus on the things most important to your cycle's success: a low-stress experience that lets your body rest, your family prepare, and your entire team work together to ensure the best possible result. The best agencies offer you relationships with every possible professional to make your experience a success along with the man power to do all of the things you couldn't possibly manage, such as donor screening, travel coordination, donor monitoring alongside your reproductive clinic, and donor education. In every sense of the word, agencies are partners with you along your journey and in our particular cases, even beyond.

If you keep in mind that agencies are here to be your partner and should, in fact, act like one, we think you'll come to understand in short order which one is the best choice from the many available. And although those in places like the United Kingdom may opt for the 100% anonymous programs offered by their national health care, we can assure you that those teams are just as committed to helping you have a positive experience as well.

A Story from Wendie

As an 12-year veteran of the egg donation industry and a multiple-time donor, one of the greatest gifts I get each day are those recipient parents who choose to stay in touch. It's a personal decision no matter how you look at it, but there's only one thing more rewarding than hearing one of our parents become pregnant from their cycle. When we receive birth announcements, photos, family newsletters, and those lovely thank you e-mails then we know we made a difference. Sure—our business is building families, but that doesn't mean we don't also love to see them grow!

CAN YOU HELP US UNDERSTAND THE DONOR'S SIDE OF OUR STORY?

Egg donors come in as many iterations as people themselves, and we can tell you, without question, that we feel there is a great donor out there to be matched with every possible intended parent. You know why you've picked up this book, but let's talk for a bit about what's going on behind the scenes with your donor and what her possible motivations are to help you along in your journey.

As the average donor compensation in the United States is between $5,000–$10,000 and in the United Kingdom a mere £250 (less than $500 at the writing of this book), the fees that donors generally receive aren't considered coercive or so much that she would consider doing something she ordinarily would not in exchange for compensation. As donors ourselves, we can tell you that the average donor fee is great for paying off student loans, credit card bills, or saving some money for a down payment on a house. Both of us have had *hyperstimulated ovaries* (a rare condition experienced by donors where the ovaries fill up with an excess of fluid, causing it to leak into the abdominal cavity—quite uncomfortable and sometimes requiring minor outpatient surgery to correct). Wendie has experienced *ovarian torsion* (where the ovary spins on its axis, cutting off blood flow). We've both driven and flown thousands of miles for monitoring, doctor's appointments, retrieval procedures, and medication pickups. So is it the money? Not in most cases. Although there are donors out there motivated by donor fee alone, most donors are like us—we heard about egg donation, researched it, went through the screening process, and ended up being selected by recipients. There was something other than the money that led us down that path.

To commit fully to becoming an egg donor, there almost has to be an additional, emotional motivation for these young ladies to offer their help for families like yours. Over the years, we have found that it's a delightful combination of empathy, understanding, and altruism that leads them to an egg donor program's doors. Most donors eventually want children or are already blessed with a family and thus understand the road you've taken that has led you to choosing them. We hear it time and time again from donors as well that if there were ever a reason later on in life when they couldn't have their own children, they'd be looking toward egg donation and people like us to fulfill their dreams.

A Donor's Perspective—Nichole's Story

Although I come from a remarkably close family, I decided egg donation was something I would do independently. I didn't want my mother to worry, so at first I didn't tell her about it. However, I ultimately decided that this was too important not to share with her. When I told her, she panicked. She confessed that although she understood what an extraordinary gift it was to help someone have a child, she needed me to understand that I was her child first and that she would do everything in her power to protect me. She forbid me from doing anything that involved any risk to my health. I assured her that the risk was quite low, that the doctors my agency works with are the best in the field, and that I had done my research. I explained that although I am nowhere near ready to be a mother myself, my body already possesses the ability to make a child, and my spirit harbors an innate happiness, unshakable enthusiasm for life, and fundamental sense of gratitude. Isn't it logical that I would want to share this with a special family?

She asked me for a few days to think it over and do her own research. She reached out to all of our relatives in the medical field, used every contact she had, and, finally, determined that the procedure is safe. She called me crying, explaining that I consistently inspire her in new ways. I told her it was she and my father who had inspired me to be loving and kind and to be the type of person who would readily offer to give that which they had to give.

In every instance in my life where I have set out to give, I've always felt as though I've ended up receiving far more. This experience was no different. My recipient mother's heartfelt words shared with me through the agency made it all beyond worth it. I read her words to my mother as well. What a miracle it is to not only be able to verbally acknowledge but to also show with action the appreciation I have for all that she and my father have given me (through both genes and nurturing), and to share this with a special woman who now has a beautiful little boy because of my decision to be a part of this journey.

BUT WILL MY DONOR FEEL AS IF THE BABY IS HERS?

While we can't speak on behalf of every woman who has chosen to be an egg donor, we can tell you the universal response from every donor we have asked over the past 12 years: Absolutely not. All of the legal paperwork and relinquishing of rights aside, your donor is looking at her donation as a genetic helping hand. A gift . . . to you. The dreams of having this child are yours, and your donor is dreaming of having children one day with her partner or by whatever means she chooses. In many cases, we find ourselves speaking with donors who have their own fears that the child's intended parents might want something from him or her in the future, asking if they will have future financial or emotional obligations to the children that are a result of their donation(s). So you see, the fears from both sides are, in actuality, rather complementary in nature.

One of my donors had the rare yet rewarding experience of not only meeting but holding the two little girls who were a result of her egg donation. She said that she is asked all the time if she feels as though she is the "mom" to these children or was that "weird" for her. This is her response:

> I can tell you with the utmost certainty there is no attachment whatsoever to the children that resulted from my egg donations. Meeting and holding them felt a lot like holding a friend's baby—you know it's not yours, nor is there any kind of bond that takes place in such a short amount of time. I don't covet them in any way, nor have I ever once thought of them as "my" children, regardless of the DNA I've contributed. There was nothing negative about meeting them. In fact, I was elated for the parents, as I could see the joy on their faces and feel the warmth emanating from them. It was a very special experience, meeting these children, as I know that most donors never have this opportunity.

WHAT DO WE NEED TO REMEMBER?

The most important thing to remember at this point in your journey is that there are numerous options available to you for building your family. There are many egg donation agencies and IVF clinics to choose from across the United States. From the 1970s until today, reproductive technology has seen so many inroads that your chances for success are better than ever. And although not everything works the first time (as we are all well aware), there are more possibilities than ever for making your dreams come true. We think it's best said by one of Wendie's clients who called her after speaking with a friend who had used donor eggs to have her son. She had asked her friend, "How did you get such an amazing child?"

To which the happy mother lovingly replied, "Science!"

Key Chapter Highlights—The Basics of Egg Donation

- **First pregnancy from IVF:** 1977

- **First pregnancy from egg donation:** 1983

- **Reproductive endocrinologist:** Doctors having earned very specific certification for OB/GYNs from the American Board of Obstetrics and Gynecology (a U.S. certifying professional organization for medical professionals).

- **Average U.S. clinic live birth rates for donor egg procedures:** 55% (2008)

- **Average U.K. clinic live birth rates for donor egg procedures:** 28.5% (2008)

- Donors are invested in your dream of becoming parents.

- Egg donor agencies are your partner in your journey.

- **Most common technologies seen in egg donor cycles:** intracytoplasmic sperm injection (ICSI), blastocysts, vitrification, preimplantation genetic diagnosis (PGD)

2

Considering Egg Donation—
Filling Your Nest

"When I found out that I could not get pregnant with my own eggs, I was devastated. I will never forget the drive home after I had been told that I would probably have to use donor eggs if I wanted to biologically conceive. I was crying so hard that I had to pull over because I couldn't see through the tears. I had fooled myself that my youthfulness and fertility would continue into my late 40s. What was wrong with me? Why couldn't I do this? I suddenly felt like a failure as a woman at my very core." —Susan

For women, there's no simple or comforting way to face being told that something in your body isn't working properly. We go through our lives seeing the women around us becoming pregnant, starting families; and the women we see in the egg donation industry are no different. One day, the information that you can't have children "the good old-fashioned way" is staring you in the face morning, noon, and night. It really doesn't matter what the reason is—age, previous cancer treatment, early menopause, or any number of other reasons women come face to face with infertility. You're facing infertility, you've been told that egg donation is something to consider and now . . . well, now you have to come to terms with the options available to you if you want to have children.

We'll begin by saying that today's culture is much different from the one in which our mothers and fathers grew up. Women have careers, more and more men are becoming stay-at-home fathers, and the media is portraying parenthood at later ages as commonplace. It's only natural that you ask *"Why is this happening to me?"* when you see every celebrity under the sun having children in their 40s and everyone around you seems to be able to get pregnant without all these trips to the doctor's office. What we've found is that not nearly enough information is available to or shared with women regarding the

9

norms of fertility and age. Although fashion and pop culture magazines help celebrities share the joys of their newfound parenthood with fans across the globe, we can say with certainty that many of those children are the gift of donor eggs. Every donor and recipient couple we've had the joy of working with over the years is most certainly assured of their privacy, but we look forward to the day when one or even several of these high-profile personalities share with the world that their family joy resulted from the gift of an egg donor.

Should you beat yourself up for having "plumbing" that is uncooperative? Certainly not. Life hands us lemons and although the most inspirational sources tell us to go ahead and make lemonade, we have a better idea: use those lemons to make a family. Although our lifestyles and culture might be much different than that of our parents, we've got one thing on our side that they did not—reproductive technology.

THE FACTS BEHIND FERTILITY

We'll begin with a simple fact: infertility isn't just a woman's concern. Low motility, nonviable sperm, previous vasectomies, and other situations place otherwise healthy men in a position where they, too, must face the reality for the need for an extra helping hand. Single and gay men are invariably faced with needing an egg donor to fulfill their dreams of family. So ladies, it's not just you. Maybe you're part of a relationship facing male factor infertility in addition to needing an egg donor. But you're not alone, and nor will you ever be in the circles of reproductive medicine.

Women who will need to seek out egg donors steadily increases as they approach their late 30s and early 40s. Vicken Sahakian, MD, of Pacific Fertility Center in Los Angeles, California, told us (without mincing any words), "I'm more likely to get pregnant than a woman over the age of 47." It's a reality that women's bodies have been producing eggs for upward of twenty years by the time we see our mid-30s and menopause is on the horizon. There's no judgment on why you decided to wait to start your family until now—there's just the understanding that others just like you are looking at the same numbers and same options. Unfortunately, the human body doesn't have one of those buttons like a holiday turkey. Nothing "pops up" when your body is done being fertile, so the reproductive industry finds many people completely blindsided when they discover things aren't working the way they should.

The quote at the beginning of this chapter reinforces something that more women facing infertility feel than not: that she is a failure at her very core for not being able to get pregnant, much less with her own eggs. However, it's hard for us to consider women failures for finding out their eggs aren't making the grade in the IVF lab. Age-related decline is not a disease that just affects *some* women, like breast cancer, arthritis, or lupus. It is a condition that will affect every single woman in the world at some point—and most of them within the same age range. It is a female condition that doesn't take into account when you meet your perfect partner or one that can be put on hold while you dive full force into a career that lets you come up for air in your 40s. It doesn't care when you are mentally, physically, or emotionally ready to build a family and could care less if you've already had children the "old-fashioned" way.

However, we understand that you're going to face those who don't understand your struggle or situation. Numbers aside, let's talk about the things you might have heard or are bound to hear.

DESTINY

They mean well, but the folks who pop up and say that perhaps it wasn't your destiny to become a parent can actually do more harm than the inspiring message they believe they're delivering. Although life takes its twists and turns, the urge to become a parent is inarguable for those who feel it. Men might want to throttle their golf buddy and ladies might end a lunch early when they hear sentiments about how others feel your infertility is a message from another source. The good news? Egg donors have chosen their own destiny, and it's to help people like you. You can thank your lucky stars for the egg donors and all of the people who work in reproductive medicine that they've chosen paths dedicated to helping people like you. And as two of those people, we wouldn't trade our paths for the world.

WHY DON'T YOU ADOPT?

There is much soul searching that happens prior to a decision to have a child through egg donation. During that process, it is possible that your family and other loved ones might wonder why you're exploring a medical solution when adoption seems to be the logical answer—at least to them. What is important to remember is that regardless of the process you choose to build your family, it is your family's decision (though many will have opinions).

Many families exploring egg donation decide to simultaneously register for adoption waiting lists. On the other side of the coin, many families that find that egg donation isn't ultimately the family building solution they hoped will turn to adoption to fulfill their dreams. It's a loving process that matches children with willing families every day. In the United States alone, over 120,000 children find homes through the adoption process each year.

If you should decide that adoption is an option you would like to pursue, we recommend the following adoption resources:

Child Welfare Information Gateway
http://www.childwelfare.gov/adoption

International Adoption Resources
http://internationaladoptionresources.org

Adopting.org
http://www.adopting.org

ISN'T IT GOING TO BE WEIRD TO CARRY SOMEONE ELSE'S BABY?

We have two takes on this. We've never once in our collective experiences working with intended parents heard of a recipient mother who felt that a child in her womb is anything but hers. The other side to this? If you know you'll be using a surrogate, you'll be following the pregnancy as if it was your own and that child will be delivered to your arms as it enters the world. It might be weird for other people to think of using donor eggs and possibly a surrogate, but we've never heard of a new mother looking at a child brought by the miracle of egg donation and thinking thoughts that were filled with anything other than love.

One of the most important things to remember is that you're not alone in your quest to have a family. Most women feel very isolated when they first discover that "letting go" of their own genetics is a part of the journey involved in egg donation. And we're here to tell you—if you're like one of Wendie's clients who shut herself in her house for almost three weeks straight because it seemed like every time she walked outside she saw pregnant women or babies—there's nothing out of the ordinary about that. Fortunately, there are thousands of others who have expanded their hearts and minds to the idea of a different way of achieving their much dreamed of families and are now proud and incomprehensibly happy parents. The question is, how do you get from how you are feeling now, to the point of letting go, accepting, and then moving forward?

SURRENDERING YOURSELF: THE FIRST STEP

Friends and family mean well, but there are no tidbits of misguided advice like those mentioned earlier, or magical words of wisdom that will help either a man or a woman understand the limits of his or her own body except the wisdom of his or her own heart. To be open to the gifts of egg donation takes a certain level of surrender, no matter your gender. In working with intended parents as they begin to explore egg donation, we've found that the best (and most well-received) advice has always been to consider the possibility of letting go of something that you cannot control in favor of focusing your energy on something you can. In the case of parents considering egg donation, that's the donor selection process, which we'll cover in-depth in Chapter 6. Along the way, you might even find it helpful to work with one of the many licensed social workers and therapists who have chosen to specialize in reproductive medicine. They work with fertility-challenged individuals and couples on a regular basis and are an excellent source of information, guidance, and solace. You can consult the American Society for Reproductive Medicine (ASRM) website (www.ASRM.org) for their more comprehensive list. Your reproductive clinic and/or donor agency will also most certainly have local resources they can recommend and share.

Abigail Glass, an experienced reproductive therapist with whom we'll be hearing from more throughout the book, shares her perspective on working with families as they let go of having a child who is genetically theirs.

> When women are faced with moving from their "biological link" or their "genetics" to "new genetics," I help them identify what those terms actually mean to them. We all grew up with some fantasies about what our family would look like and how it would get created and what a "mini me" would look/be like. Often, people go through a process of grieving the loss of these fantasies. However, when women (and men) actually answer these questions of what biological link and genetics means to them, they begin to realize that once they have a child, however that happens, they end up having the connections they yearn for and have been in fear of not getting. The process just looks different. This is also a spiritual journey or teaching for many people. When someone is able to see the larger spiritual perspective, they can begin to see the ways we are all connected.

THE MYTH OF CONTROL

Remember those picture-perfect scenarios where people who want to have children can just miraculously have them (and on the first try)? You know as well as we do that those scenarios are things of the movies and not what you're dealing with. Whether you're a same-sex couple struggling with the need to use eggs or sperm that aren't from either partner or already have children of your own and wanting to further build your family, the challenges are all the same. And they are factors that are, as we've well realized, out of our control.

Your life has come to a beautiful place, one where you want to add children to it and continue to grow not just your own life, but someone else's as well. But did you ever imagine you would be here? This book is a guide to help people of all walks of life through the "what to expect when you weren't expecting this" scenario (one that's probably more familiar to you these days than any other). As much as we can control the behavior of the driver in the car next to us on the freeway—that's about as much control as men and women have over their own fertility. Fertility therapist Brenda Hart-Fahn, MFT, says it beautifully.

> One of the lessons that most women and couples have to learn when going through infertility is that only so much of life and what happens is in one's control. Trying to control life is usually an illusion anyway, so I talk to women about working on letting go and living in the moment, as most of our fears never come to fruition. If any parent would sit down and think of all the possible scenarios that could happen regarding having children, no one would ever want to become a parent! I talk to parents about the role of attachment to one's child and that regardless if a parent becomes a parent through adoption, IVF, ovum donation or surrogacy, what is important is being attuned and attached to whoever that child is. Children will thrive when they feel loved, seen and heard for who they are, not because of how they came to be.

As you think of your own doubts, fears, and attachments, think of what you can let go. How will your life be richer for what you don't carry with you as you explore the ways you can build your family? Assisted reproductive technology has made astounding strides over the past decade and stands poised to make even more, so falling in love with your options like egg donation is a sound choice and the ultimate goal of your journey.

An Exercise in Letting Go—One Couple's Journey

Tom and Maria (names have been changed) struggled with infertility for several years before finally realizing and accepting that having a biological child was a slim possibility. They would need to explore egg donation, and it was advised as a viable solution to prevent further frustrations and strains on their finances. They started working with a therapist who was helping them let go of the *idea* of their unborn child that they were going to have together. Tom and Maria each wrote letters that covered everything they had fantasized about, from whose eyes the baby would have to whether or not he or she would be artistic, athletic, academic, or otherwise. They then took a long hike and found a private place with a beautiful view. They each read their letter aloud to the other. Once they were done, they burned the letters and let the ashes float over the hilltop. They both found this remarkably healing and the first major step toward parenting the child they were meant to have.

WHEN WILL I BE ABLE TO MOVE FORWARD?

It doesn't matter where you are in your journey toward having a family—you could be just starting off or a gay couple continuously challenged with finding resources and professionals who work with alternative families. The first thing to remember is that there is no set timeline for how long it will take you to be ready for the next step. Everyone goes about the egg donor process differently (and that includes the donors as well). We've worked with women who have called the same afternoon they were told by their doctor that they couldn't use their own eggs and are ready to begin the process immediately. They all seem to gain hope and inspiration from looking at donor profiles and seeing who they feel they'd want as friends or otherwise feel connected to. They also usually choose an egg donor in a fairly short amount of time. It's a combination of grieving and progress, where they use one process to cope with and reconcile another.

On the opposite end of the spectrum, it's not uncommon for Wendie's agency to receive calls from women who are emotionally distressed and overwhelmed by the process of choosing a donor. That's a perfectly normal response. In these cases, it's not uncommon for these women to work with a reproductive therapist to help them come to terms that will allow them to move forward and select an egg donor. Strength is key; as is hope. We find that most women are somewhere in the middle of this spectrum. Carole Lieber Wilkins, a well-known marriage and family therapist specializing in infertility and reproductive medicine and parent to one of the first 11 children born via egg donation in the United States, offers this to those who wonder about the time it takes to be "ready" to move forward with egg donation: "There is no particular time frame. Some women are ready to move forward in a few weeks, some in a few years. For some, letting go of their genetic offspring is more difficult than for others. However long it takes to be fully ready, take the time. In the long run, the preparation will be well worth it. The decisions in family building are too important to rush."

Brenda Hardt-Fahn, MFT, explains her process for helping families move through the initial shock.

> It's always hard to generalize how a woman will feel or react to the news that she needs an egg donor. Yet there are common themes that come up for women: feelings of disappointment, anger, helplessness, inadequacy. At times women may feel some ambivalence to whether they want to proceed with a donor because they are emotionally spent from years of the ups and downs of trying to become pregnant. Frequently, women will wonder if they are up for jumping into another infertility approach. What I encourage all women to do is feel their feelings, regardless of what those feelings may be. If she

tries to deny her feelings, those feelings will manifest in other ways (depression, anxiety, physical symptoms, lack of energy). A woman needs to go through her own grief process of realizing that her child will not be her genetic child. Following that process, she can then accept the reality of her situation and hopefully accept the reality of who she is, complete with her beauty, limitations and faults, and realize that life is perfect when you can accept the imperfections of life.

What we want to instill most is that through all of the emotional mud and muck, hope emerges as something that you can't lose sight of. We see it time and again, and although there are those who might plant a seed of doubt, the only people on the journey you're taking are the ones who truly stand to benefit from the joys of the family you seek to create.

A BIT ABOUT THE NAYSAYERS

The unfortunate and, again, insensitive negative press that egg donation, surrogacy, and other infertility treatments receive can be disheartening if you're beginning to explore your options. We think that part of the beauty of humankind is that we all share unique thoughts and beliefs. On occasion, those with thoughts and beliefs opposed to the advances in reproductive medicine speak loudly and are, quite frankly, uninvited. Regardless of their motivations, they speak out against the options you have available to you, and we think it's best to address those here in the most impartial manner possible so if you haven't faced these arguments, you're aware they exist.

Whether their voices are driven by religious faith or some other moral base, it's important to know that no one understands your journey better than you. The love you'll have for your child, whether you conceive through egg donation, require a surrogate, are building a household that others consider to be outside the norm (i.e., a same-sex couple or a single-parent family) is no different than the love any other parent will have for their child.

There are those blessed with coming by family with little to no help from technology, and then there are others who are grateful for every ounce of technology available for their journey. The bottom line is this: there will always be those who judge others for their actions. We fully respect the right for others to believe what they will about the miracles of modern medical technology and to practice those beliefs with their own families and in their own lives. We hope that you, the intended parents reading this book, will be free from the stresses of those who don't agree with your decisions for one reason or another and hope that the naysayers will discover the beauty in a moment of silence as they watch other human beings reach for the joys they already know and experience: those of family.

WHERE TO FIND RESOURCES

When the time is right and should you need them, there are thousands of fertility professionals who work with people facing situations similar to yours each day. To find therapists who are qualified and experienced in the field of infertility, you can

- contact RESOLVE (www.resolve.org), a national fertility support group with locations across the United States
- contact PVED (Parents Via Egg Donation—www.pved.org), one of the largest nonprofit organizations for those facing infertility and exploring egg donation
- visit the ASRM (American Society for Reproductive Medicine—www.asrm.org), as they have a host of resources from specialty therapists to fertility clinics and donor agencies
- consult the SART (Society for Assisted Reproductive Technology—www.sart.org) for everything including member professionals, clinic statistics, donor agencies, and other fertility-related resources
- ask your reproductive clinic for a list of therapists they can recommend
- speak with your egg donor agency, if you've already chosen one. Most agencies have a list of select therapist they've worked with on a regular basis and can give you recommended professionals to explore

WHAT DO WE NEED TO REMEMBER?

Never hesitate to ask for help on your journey toward becoming a parent. There are so many people, from other men and women just like you to professionals who have dedicated their lives to building families that you should never feel you're at a loss for resources. While the naysayers will always be there, there's one thing that can never be argued: today's medical technology offers you the greatest possibility of achieving your family dreams, and more so than any other time in history. We'll say these are pretty good times to live in, wouldn't you?

Key Chapter Highlights—Considering Egg Donation

Organizations you can contact for referrals:

- **RESOLVE** (www.resolve.org)—Because one in eight people of childbearing age faces fertility challenges, this national nonprofit organization is dedicated to providing education and resources pertaining to fertility. They offer extensive online resources ranging from articles to webinars and podcasts to a complete professional services directory where you can find everything from therapists who specialize in fertility issues to egg donor agencies and reproductive clinics in your area.

- **PVED** (www.pved.org)—Parents Via Egg Donation is the only national nonprofit organization dedicated to gathering resources for those seeking information and support as they explore egg donation. They have an extensive members' forum where you can communicate directly with other intended parents and get referrals for every reproductive professional possible, from egg donor agencies to attorneys and fertility therapists.

- **ASRM** (www.asrm.org)—Offers comprehensive lists of resources ranging from agencies, clinics, and other fertility professionals.

- **SART** (www.sart.org)—A powerful resource for clinic statistics, egg donor agency referrals, and other professionals in the fertility industry for intended parents to explore.

3

Beyond the Nest—When Hearts and Science Collide

For any woman who has faced fertility challenges, there comes a point when you must ask yourself, "When is enough *enough*?" That is, when do you stop looking for your body to perform and start asking for outside help from the assisted reproductive medical community? The answer is different for every man and woman and as you may well know, sperm and eggs alike don't come with an expiration date on their container.

Although you might see people around you every day starting families the "old-fashioned way," there comes a time when medical professionals should ethically (and compassionately) recommend that you seek an egg donor to improve your chances for achieving pregnancy. In this chapter, we'll explore the recommendations and experiences from multiple, well-known reproductive endocrinologists. Our goal is to give you a solid base of information from which you cannot only use to ask better questions of your own fertility team, but to also make the best decisions possible for your personal fertility scenario.

YOUR EGGS VERSUS DONOR EGGS—WHEN SHOULD YOU LET GO AND LET SCIENCE?

It's never an easy decision to consider "abandoning" your own genetics and opting to use an egg donor, and we know you're no stranger to hearing, "Well, you just have to keep trying!" However, there comes a point in some women's journey through assisted reproduction where it is inadvisable, from both a financial and pragmatic standpoint, to continue cycling with your own eggs. So how do you know the "when" has come for you and your fertility specialist to consider egg donation as a viable alternative?

In interviewing the many doctors Wendie has worked with over the years, she uncovered some common responses that we'll share here. According to these physicians, it's most commonly recommended that women stop cycling with their own eggs when and if they

- have diagnosed ovarian failure
- are older than the age of 42
- have FSH (follicle-stimulating hormone) levels greater than 15 mIU/mL during cycles with their own eggs
- have history of poor response to stimulating medications
- have history of two to three failed IVF cycles with their own eggs
- have history of chromosomal issues (e.g., translocations or inversions)
- have history of genetic or autosomal dominant problems (see Glossary)

Of course, we've all heard the miracle stories about a woman getting pregnant with her own eggs against all odds, but your reproductive specialist will tell you when it's time to begin considering alternatives. That time will be different for every woman, so you can find comfort in proceeding at your own pace. In fact, many of Wendie's intended mothers have opted to cycle an additional time with their own eggs and admittedly without much hope, but it was the action they needed to be able to confidently move forward with egg donation in the future.

Some intended mothers find, because of special circumstances such as early menopause or a history of ovarian cancer, the decision to use an egg donor is their only option for building their family. Even in these cases, the decision to let go and let science lend a helping hand isn't necessarily easy. The same emotional turmoil can take over and make you wonder about the one in a million stories you see on television and read in magazines. Why can't that be me? Isn't there something that can help me build the family of my dreams using my own eggs? We recommend consulting with your fertility specialist and a counselor experienced with reproductive challenges to help you work through not only your options but also the emotions that accompany them.

WHAT DO THE DOCTORS SAY?

We've been fortunate to be on the giving side of the assisted reproductive industry, helping those who need egg donors achieve their dreams. From a personal standpoint, you're reading the words of two women who understand the gift of egg donation equally with the reality that you never thought you'd be reading this book in a million years. Wendie's worked with many of the top reproductive endocrinologists in the nation through the thousands of egg donor cycles she's coordinated, so we turned to them to offer their insights on advising patients to explore egg donation.

Vicken Sahakian, MD, board-certified reproductive endocrinologist and fertility specialist, from Pacific Fertility Center (Los Angeles, California)

The transition to egg donation is a difficult one for most patients, especially women still in their reproductive prime. In general, women over the age of 43 have a very small chance of conceiving using their own eggs. Therefore, I typically discourage women older than 44 to attempt IVF using their own eggs, especially if they would suffer financially if they fail. Some younger women will unfortunately also have to resort to egg donation as their only hope of becoming parents, short of adoption. These cases are usually much tougher, as these patients will have a harder time accepting this option given their age. Typically, if a woman responds poorly to fertility hormones or produces poor quality eggs on at least two successive IVF cycles, I will also recommend egg donation. My practice is committed to helping women from all walks of life build their families, so I suggest to these women that they focus on that goal instead of the obstacle their eggs are presenting. Egg donation is a wonderful alternative to getting these women to their goals.

Greg Rosen, MD, board-certified reproductive endocrinologist and fertility specialist, from Reproductive Partners Medical Group, Inc. (Beverly Hills, California) and coauthor of What He Can Expect When She's Not Expecting *(Skyhorse Publishing, 2011)*

The single most important thing for women to recognize is that when a woman ages, so do her eggs! Women are born with a certain number of eggs and there's nothing that can make them create any more. In fact, the two biggest predictors of a woman's ability to conceive are her age and how long she has been trying. Women are most fertile between ages 22 and 24 years, and then the percentage of women who are able to conceive declines while the chance that she may miscarry increases. By age 40, over one-half of women are still able to conceive; but by age 45, fewer than one in eight women are able to both conceive and carry. Miscarriages, usually a sign that the egg fertilized was not healthy enough to allow a normal child to be born, increase from 9% at peak fertility in a woman's early 20s to 50% by age 42–45.

In other words, women usually lose the ability to have a child about 10 years before their last period (the onset of menopause). The average age for menopause is between the ages of 51 and 52 years, but there are a number of health issues that are associated with premature destruction of woman's eggs. Some are medical (surgery, chemotherapy, radiation therapy, etc.), and some are genetic (your family's genetic history, Turner's syndrome, to name a few).

So who is a candidate for using egg donation to help have a child? This is an incredibly difficult question to answer. In my mind, there are only two unequivocal requirements: (1) emotional closure on your desire to have a child only with our own eggs, and (2) you must be healthy enough to become pregnant, carry the pregnancy and deliver, and healthy enough to be a mother and raise the child. Closure is so important and is frequently overlooked by both patients and practitioner as we're all looking for ways to move forward. What's important to remember is that, while most women who conceive with donor eggs will have *some* regrets about their lack of genetics in their child, these regrets are short-lived and easily controlled with their acceptance that their pregnancy and child are the result of using the incredibly powerful and readily available resources of egg donation to reach their goals.

Bradford Kolb, MD, board-certified reproductive endocrinologist and fertility specialist, from Huntington Reproductive Center (Los Angeles, California)

It is crucial that physicians take time to learn about their patient's hopes, desires, and expectations. This process seldom takes place in a single visit as it is necessary to learn about each patient's history, run appropriate tests, and educate them about treatment options. Personally, I offer each patient as much time reviewing their prognosis, treatment options, realistic prognosis, and costs as they need. Often, the news that patients may need an egg donor is a new and scary event. Many patients embrace the hope offered by fertility treatment. Often, women with poor egg quality will pursue treatment with their own eggs before considering egg donation or adoption. This approach can be quite therapeutic as it allows them the opportunity to feel that they have done everything possible prior to pursuing egg donation and then move forward with confidence. Some patients choose to pursue egg donation while others may choose adoption or a life without children. With time and careful guidance, most patients will be able to find a path that best fits their personal needs. I'm always happy to be a part of that process, whichever path it follows.

The important thing to remember is, as these industry experts have demonstrated, the process is different for each woman but there are shared experiences. Acceptance is key, and most physicians will openly share their insights with you on when they feel that proceeding with your own eggs might prove futile. Be open to having a candid dialogue with your chosen reproductive specialist, as we've heard time and time again from intended mothers that the candor of their chosen fertility doctors was the trigger that led them down the road to egg donation and, in many cases, helped build the family they live with and love today.

THE NEXT STEP: REASONS TO CONTINUE EXPLORING EGG DONATION

Up until now, you've probably had your fair share of medical mumbo jumbo thrown around. But what about the emotional side of choosing egg donation as the means for creating your family? You're no stranger to the fact that medical technology offers some extremely powerful assistance to help people build families, but technical terms aside, it's time to discuss *you*.

If you have insurance or expendable income that helps cover the costs of repeated IVF cycles along with the emotional endurance needed to rise above yet another negative pregnancy test, there's probably little anyone can do to keep you from cycling one more time with your own eggs. For most people, however, both finances and emotions become exhausted and the point comes when you must decide if you want to be a parent or if you want to be a parent only if there can be a genetic link between you and your child(ren).

Thinking of this from yet another perspective, do you know a family member or close friend who has a child(ren) for whom you'd simply do anything? Perhaps you have a special bond with them. Now, imagine that you suddenly became the parent to this child. Would you feel any less like their mom or dad if you had to take on that role? Would you love them any less? The point is our capacity to love and be a parent to a child comes from within our own hearts, not our genetics.

If you're able to recognize your ability to love a child that comes into your life without a genetic bond, then the next step is determining how you'll move forward with the process. We like to call this part "letting go and letting science." When you're emotionally ready to take the next step, reproductive technology will be ready and waiting with open arms.

ETHICAL CONSIDERATIONS FOR EGG DONATION

The American Society for Reproductive Medicine (ASRM) has assembled an ethics committee report discussing the various guidelines by which they feel all egg donation agencies and IVF clinics should abide. It is important to note that these are guidelines and not laws, so you will need to consider how important each guideline is to you and how important it is for the egg donation agency or IVF clinic you work with to abide by them. In our experience, most agencies and clinics do their best to follow most of the guidelines, making exceptions for certain cases or unique situations.

There are three guidelines that are discussed most, so we'll lend our focus to those in the words that follow. (For a complete list of ethical considerations for third-party reproduction, please visit www.ASRM.org.) Those three are egg donor compensation, recommended age for egg donors, and the maximum number of cycles per egg donor. Let's explore these three in more depth.

Donor Compensation

Of these three, the most talked about and discussed guideline (and certainly the one that brings the most scrutiny to our industry) is donor compensation. In the United Kingdom, egg donor compensation is minimal (less than $500 at the writing of this book). As we've discussed previously and will cover in more detail in Chapter 6, the average egg donor compensation in the United States ranges between $5,000–$10,000 per cycle. Given that information, let's have a look at the ASRM guidelines for donor compensation[7]*:

- Financial compensation of women donating oocytes for infertility therapy or for research is justified on ethical grounds.

- Compensation should be structured to acknowledge the time, inconvenience, and discomfort associated with screening, ovarian stimulation, and oocyte retrieval. Compensation should not vary according to the planned use of the oocytes, the number or quality of oocytes retrieved, the number or outcome of prior donation cycles, or the donor's ethnic or other personal characteristics.

- Total payments to donors in excess of $5,000 require justification and sums above $10,000 are not appropriate.

- To discourage inappropriate decisions to donate oocytes, programs should adopt effective information disclosure and counseling processes. Donors independently recruited by prospective oocyte recipients or agencies should undergo the same disclosure and counseling process as donors recruited by the program.

- Oocyte-sharing programs should formulate and disclose clear policies on the eligibility criteria for participants and on how oocytes will be allocated, especially if a low number of oocytes or oocytes of varying quality are produced.

- Treating physicians owe the same duties to oocyte donors as to any other patients. Programs should ensure equitable and fair provision of services to donors.

- Programs should adopt and disclose policies regarding coverage of an oocyte donor's medical costs should she experience complications from the procedure.

The theory behind a fee exceeding $10,000 is that the ASRM feels fees that high could potentially be coercive, or motivate a potential donor to ignore the risks associated with egg donation in exchange for the financial compensation. Although most donors that we have worked with over the years take the time to ask numerous questions of both our office and the doctor's office prior to committing to this process, there is certainly no doubt that there were and always will be some who are more motivated by the financial reward to the point of not performing the suggested education regarding the overall risk. However, it would be more fair to give the majority of these young women far more credit when it comes to making the decision to donate eggs. Although the allure of compensation can offer certain levels of motivation, we can attest that as multiple-time donors as well as people who have worked with numerous donors throughout the years that most of them are able to decide whether or not the financial gain is worth the physical risk. Our personal motivations as well as the ones we've heard most frequently from donors are that although the financial compensation is a pleasant reward, the most pleasant would be the knowledge that other people will benefit from our donation.

We think the most important thing to remember is that there are donors available well within the ASRM compensation guidelines. Higher fees will generally be seen for multiple-time donors with proven pregnancies and intended parent deliveries, although this isn't the only reason a donor's fee exceeds the $5,000–$10,000 threshold.

As a general rule, first-time donor fees range between $5,000–$6,000. These young ladies, although willing to share an incredible gift, are unproven and intended parents are hoping that everything will go as planned with their stimulation cycle and retrieval. In Chapter 6, we'll discuss in more detail choosing your egg donor and the financial implications attached to the process. In the end, you have to feel comfortable with not only your donor, but also the costs associated with each donor. You will always be the best judge of your financial and emotional limits.

But what about donors who do receive higher compensation than the ASRM guidelines indicate? Those who run egg donor agencies have been put in a difficult position when it comes to donors who possess characteristics that are in high demand or difficult to find in the egg donor population as a whole. We want to make it clear that these donors are not being judged as "better." Rather, if someone is on the varsity gymnastics team in college and the intended mother was as well (and athletic ability has been designated by an intended parent as a highly important factor in choosing a donor), that would be a more difficult person to find. Thus, if a donor comes into an agency roster with this unique characteristic or others like it, what is the agency obligation to the intended parent?

At Wendie's agency, she will let the intended parent know that this donor has her exact requirements but is asking an unusually high compensation. Knowing that this type of donor is not easy to find, the decision is ultimately left to the intended parent and Wendie will make alternate donor recommendations featuring young women who meet a significant number of the intended parent criteria but whose fees are considerably less than this seemingly exclusive donor.

This particular situation, where a donor possess characteristics in particular or high demand, leads to the that an unregulated cap in the donor egg industry will cause donors to demand fees of $20,000, $30,000, or even $50,000. This fear, in Wendie's experience, is unwarranted for several reasons. First and foremost, there are far more egg donors listed with the various agencies across the country than will ever be chosen by recipient parents. Most of which could not command $30,000, much less $10,000, as there simply isn't the demand. For example, there are probably a few thousand cute, athletic college students who have applied to be egg donors all across America. If one of these young women decided that she wanted a fee of $20,000, what are the chances that someone will pay her that when they can find someone very similar who is only asking $5,000–$10,000?

The handful of donors who have cycled for exceptionally high donor fees are few and far between. You'll find them in your journey if you look hard enough, but they represent such a minority in our industry as a whole that it is hardly worth worrying about. Most donors, even highly educated or those with seemingly exceptional characteristics, are willing to accept a first-time donor fee well within the ASRM guidelines. We are firmly of the belief that money does not give you access to a better donor. Rather, it grants access to donors in unique situations to demand higher fees due to particular traits.

For more guidance and conversation on egg donor compensation, you can seek out numerous support groups or Web sites where other intended parents go to discuss their journey throughout this process. Inevitably, you will hear of someone who paid a donor what they feel is an extraordinarily high fee for her attributes and/or a successful previous cycle, only to find out that theirs did not result in a pregnancy. Or the donor took her medication incorrectly. Or any number of other reasons why the cycle was unsuccessful. For this reason, we suggest not limiting yourself and your resources to a donor who is demanding anything you consider to be an uncomfortable fee unless you have expendable income and a strong emotional constitution. In all the agencies across the United States, if you can only find one donor who fits your checklist and that donor is requesting a compensation of $30,000, then perhaps that's a good time to stop, take a deep breath, and reevaluate what it means to be a parent and what is most important to you on your journey to family. In our opinion, there is not an egg donor on the planet unique enough to command $30,000. Although we are in favor of egg donors being compensated appropriately for their time, efforts, and priceless gift, the fact of the matter is that this is not a guaranteed process. You cannot draw up a contract stating that the donor gets her fee only if the cycle produces a pregnancy. As long as you are healthy and your physician feels you have the option of cycling multiple times, the odds are in your favor that you will get pregnant if you choose a young, healthy donor.

As with anything in medical science, there will always be times when a cycle doesn't work for whatever reason, and that should be taken into consideration. If you put all your eggs into one basket (pun intended) with a high compensation donor and you don't become pregnant, there is no going back to recoup those funds. Wendie has worked with a number of high-profile clients over the years and can only think of only one who paid a donor more than $10,000. We say this only to reinforce the point that even if you *do* have expendable income, your donor fee is not what buys you a successful cycle.

One thing you can expect in your search for an egg donor is that if she is a previously cycled and proven donor (proven meaning that she stimulated well and produced a good cycle of eggs that became quality embryos), she will likely command a higher fee. This is due to several reasons, first of which is the risk to a donor's health may (possibly) go up with each subsequent cycle. After all, egg donation is a relatively new medical procedure in the grand scheme of things, and the long-term effects on a donor's body are still being studied. Additionally, a donor will also recognize the discomfort level or recovery time she will need to donate again and/or return to her everyday activities. Some donors bounce right back and feel great just a few days after their retrieval. Others take a much longer time to recover. The big picture is that it is worth it for the sake of helping bring joy and family to the intended parents, but the recovery reality is that it is also difficult in some cases and the lost time needs to be taken into account. Finally, a young woman who is willing to come back and help other families have children should be compensated higher for the willingness to continue to share her time, efforts, and genetics with others.

Lastly, on the subject of donor compensation, there are ethical issues stemming from the idea that eggs are something that are bought and sold in the marketplace. Some view this as "baby selling" and therefore feel that compensation limits help control this and that all agencies and IVF practices should strictly adhere to ASRM guidelines. The continued back-and-forth argument there is that it's not the eggs themselves that are being purchased. Donor compensation is for the time, effort, and discomfort involved in participating in an egg donor protocol. There are ongoing discussions in our industry on the issue of donor compensation, and although all parties will never agree on all sides of the issue, we can continue to take part in these discussions and see how they will evolve over time. It's also important to note that most agencies strive to keep within the guidelines of the ASRM when it comes to donor compensation.

Donor Age Guidelines

How old is too old to be an egg donor, and what age range is optimal in the opinion of the reproductive endocrinology community? The ASRM suggests that egg donors be between the ages of 21 and 34. Twenty-one years is the age at which the ethics committee decided a donor was old enough to give true informed consent. At 34 years, there comes a question about the added risk of genetic defects to any children born from the donor's eggs. Most IVF clinics require that an egg donor be between the ages of 21 and 32. Having worked with many different IVF clinics, Wendie has seen a wide variety in each clinic's preferred age range for donors. One doctor's office in particular feels that once a young woman turns 18, it is her option to make the choice to be an egg donor. Another office doesn't want donors to be older than 25 or younger than 21. Yet another office has no problem using a first-time donor who is 32. The stats within each office vary widely on success rates because of age, but the general consensus in the industry makes a strong case for the 21–32 age range.

But how do you solve the donor age quandary when you're selecting your egg donor? Let's say you find yourself faced with the option of selecting a donor who is 19 or 20. At this point, you need to decide whether or not you feel she is mature enough that you can comfortably move forward with her. How does your IVF clinic feel, and what are their preferred guidelines? What does your egg donor agency say regarding working with a younger donor? If you decide that this donor is a fit for your wishes, it's a great time to ask some additional questions of your agency. Did this young woman go through additional screening to determine that she's ready to accept the responsibility of the donor protocol? What additional screening was performed and by whom? Is the donor close to turning 21?

Regarding older donors (30–34 years), what does your doctor say about statistics for success compared to a donor in her 20s? Wendie's experience spans all ages of donors. For example, she worked with a donor who just turned 32 and asked to do one final donation. Her past three cycles always produced in excess of 30 eggs and every intended parent was pregnant. In this situation, if an intended parent or physician expressed concern over the donor's age, Wendie would point out that this donor had a successful cycle within the last six months, and she is likely to have another good one. It is her experience that the vast majority of IVF physicians, even those who typically prefer donors in their 20s, would find this donor to be a good candidate. Erika performed her final donor cycle when she was 32, resulting in a pregnancy and a family who now has a beautiful six-year-old daughter. Wendie did her final cycle at age 34 (as a donation for a sibling to a previous donation), resulting in a healthy baby boy. Age should not be the only factor in consideration when choosing a donor, and it's best to work with your fertility specialist to understand how a donor's age and previous cycle history (if applicable) will affect your personal scenario.

Number of Cycles: What Are the Guidelines?

By now, you're well aware that there are both first-time and repeat donors that will be available to you as you review your donor options. But how many times can an egg donor offer her gift? The ASRM guidelines indicate that the cap on the number of donations per donor should be six cycles. The reason behind this is two fold. First, because although there is currently no documented study that indicates long-term adverse effects to egg donors, this is still considered a relatively new industry. Thus, the ASRM feel it to be prudent to limit the cycles in the interests of donor safety.

Second, there is the risk (and/or fear) of too many donations raising the chances of half-siblings meeting and procreating in the future. Because the majority of egg donation cycles are still anonymous, there is the minute possibility that the children born via egg donation may not know they were conceived through donor egg. We could add a Luke/Leia *Star Wars* reference here, but in the realm of probability, it's highly unlikely. If you find yourself choosing an egg donor who is now on her seventh donation and for all intents and purposes seems like your perfect candidate, how real are these fears to you? Does the agency know if her other donations were with intended parents who live in your same area? Would it make a difference if you had a donor who has donated in various countries around the world or three other times in your state? Wendie has worked in doctor's offices that have a cap of 10 cycles per donor, whereas others have no cap so long as the donor is still responding well to the medications and has expressed an understanding of potential risks.

A SUMMARY OF THE LEADING ASRM GUIDELINES

The point for sharing these guidelines with you is to allow you to start considering what factors are the most important to you as you go through this journey. It allows you to ask better questions of your egg donation agency and IVF clinic as to why they may or may not follow each of the ASRM guidelines to a tee, and how important is that to you and your experience throughout this process. What we can tell you is that it is easy to find a donor whose fee is well within the ASRM guidelines who has donated less than the recommended six times and between the ages of 21 and 32. If your search leads you to a donor outside of these suggested guidelines, please be sure to ask questions of your agency and clinic and make sure that it's the best decision for you and your unique scenario as it's true that no donor is a one-size-fits-all solution

Key Chapter Highlights—Beyond the Nest: When Hearts and Science Collide

- Reasons intended parents need to explore egg donation:
  - They have diagnosed ovarian failure
  - They are older than the age of 42
  - FSH (follicle-stimulating hormone) levels greater than 15mIU/mL during cycles with their own eggs
  - History of poor response to stimulating medications
  - History of two to three failed IVF cycles with their own eggs
  - History of chromosomal issues (e.g., translocations or inversions)
  - History of genetic or autosomal dominant problems (see Glossary)
- Aging is a natural process—your decision to approach family building at any time in your life is your prerogative
- Average egg donor ages: 20–32
- Averages for donor compensation in the United States
  - $4,000–$7,000 per cycle
  - Fees higher than $10,000 are rare
  - Donors with rare characteristics (exceptional athletic or academic ability, for example) may command slightly higher donor fees

4

How to Choose a Reproductive Clinic

With more than 600 fertility clinics in the United States alone, where do you begin the process of finding just the right one to trust with the building of your family? When we look for a new dentist or eye doctor, the determining factor is often location, location, location. However, when it comes to something as important and life changing as putting together the team of medical professionals to help you have a baby, it's not as simple as choosing the practice closest to your home or office. The type of care, IVF cycle details, options for egg donors, and overall success rates vary widely from clinic to clinic. In this chapter, we'll explore the most common questions for intended parents and give you the tools to ask better questions as you proceed with your clinic selection.

Not unlike selecting any other medical professional, the reproductive endocrinologist who was right for a friend or fellow intended parent on an Internet support site may not be right for you. There is not a one-size-fits-all nature to this industry, but we will share that there is one common goal all intended parents should strive for: finding the fertility specialist and clinic that will make your journey as stress free as possible.

The reasons different intended parents choose one reproductive specialist and clinic over another are as wide-ranging as the number of clinics themselves. So where to begin? Over the years, Wendie has worked with so many intended parents and fertility clinics that she's able to indicate which questions arise most frequently. We'll use those as a guide to build a list to help guide you through the interview process during your clinic and specialist selection phase. Ultimately, we hope you'll have the resources at your disposal for selecting the best possible professionals to create the ideal medical side of your journey.

HOW LONG DOES IT TAKE TO GET AN APPOINTMENT? HOW WAS THEIR RESPONSE TIME IN GETTING BACK TO YOU ABOUT YOUR QUESTIONS?

This process is extremely emotional, not only for the financial burden it places on you, but also the uncertainty of the process as a whole—will you achieve pregnancy and see your dreams realized? We can't emphasize enough that you should choose to work with a clinic that is not only able to see you promptly for an initial consultation, but also able to call you back in a timely fashion when you have questions. There are certainly boundaries that must be observed when working with any clinic, as they have multiple patients and their time must be distributed among all of them fairly. However, there should never be a point where your calls aren't returned and your needs remain unmet.

We think the best way to assess how easy it will be to get in contact with your clinic should you choose to become a patient is observing their behavior from the first point of contact. Did they have time to get you in for an initial appointment within a couple of weeks, or were you on a more than six-week waiting list? If you had an appointment with a reproductive endocrinologist, did they take the time to answer all of your questions sufficiently or did you feel rushed? Was the front office staff considerate and responsive to your questions? All of these things may not feel very important at the onset in comparison with the clinic's cycle statistics, but they're huge indicators of what it will be like to experience an IVF cycle with that clinic. Just think—whether you'll be going through your first IVF cycle or fifth, there are quite a few moving parts to that equation from medications to donors to testing and procedures. If you don't feel like the office staff and a particular reproductive endocrinologist will be ready to assist you and maintain a level of communication you consider appropriate, you're just setting yourself up for unnecessary stress during a time where you need as little as possible. Regardless of how popular a clinic seems to be in the online community or among friends, there is never a point where timeliness, courtesy, and efficiency should be compromised.

ARE THE DOCTORS AT THE CLINIC BOARD CERTIFIED?

Some intended parents starting this journey are lucky and have a friend who worked with a reproductive endocrinologist with rave reviews and a successful cycle. Most people, however, are starting from scratch and using every resource imaginable to figure out which clinic to use to help them achieve the most amazing thing they could possibly imagine. Choosing a doctor based on location (however convenient) is not the only thing that should be considered. The best place to start your research is with some simple verification of medical credentials. The two most legitimate groups in the United States would be the American Board of Medical Specialties (ABMS) or American Board of Physician Specialties (ABPS). In the United Kingdom, you can consult the General Medical Council (GMC), which also has a roster of specialty physicians. There are other entities who claim to board-certify physicians; however, if they are not one of the two listed, you should do some further research to find out the validity of the certifying organization. It's not uncommon to find the following additional memberships and credentials with physicians specializing in fertility-related medicine.

- FACOG—Fellow of the American College of Obstetricians and Gynecologists
- ASRM—Member, American Society for Reproductive Medicine
- ESHRE—European Society of Human Reproduction and Embryology

HOW IMPORTANT ARE THE CLINIC'S STATISTICS?

There are roughly 600 IVF clinics in the United States, 441 of which reported their success rates to the Society for Assisted Reproductive Technologies (SART).[8] Although it is required by law for all clinics to send this information to the Centers for Disease Control and Prevention (CDC), it is not a requirement that they share these statistics with SART. SART lists the statistics from all member physicians and clinics on an annual basis, and you can review those online at their Web site (www.sart.org).

Why would some physicians choose to not report to SART? It may be caused by the multitude of variables involved in how the stats are reported. This can be confusing during your search for a clinic because many online resources for intended parents suggest that SART success rates are the single most important determining factor in choosing an IVF clinic. There is no arguing that success rates are extremely important; however, there are also other important things to note when determining which clinic you'll use to build your family. First, some clinics restrict the patients with whom they will work, which can potentially translate into higher reported pregnancy rates. Other clinics are known for their willingness to work with anybody who feels they need to "keep trying" until they are ready to try a different route. It could result in a skew in reported numbers and thus, the reluctance of some clinics to participate in SART's reporting process.

It's possible that you already have or will encounter this scenario if your particular case presents a challenge for achieving a pregnancy. For example, if you choose to use a close friend or family member as your egg donor, but they are past the age requirements for a typical donor or have a medical issue that does not make them ideal, then clinics may refuse to move forward with your case as they don't want to put you, or their statistics, in the position of a potentially negative outcome.

Wendie recently worked with an intended mother with this exact situation. She had been rejected by three clinics due to their belief that she would be unlikely to achieve pregnancy. She asked if there were any clinics Wendie knew of that would allow her to try one last time, as she felt strongly that's what she needed to move on. And indeed, there are doctors who will gladly accept a case like hers regardless of the likely negative pregnancy that would occur. Wendie was able to make a few recommendations, and the intended mother was able to pursue what she felt to be her best path.

It's also important to factor in that not all IVF clinics list each doctor's statistics individually; rather, they report them as a whole for the clinic. Thus, if Doctor A at their practice has an 85% success rate, but his partner, Doctor B has a 50% success rate, the clinic's success rates will be reported to SART as 65%. Therefore, it's important to note if you're going to cycle somewhere with multiple reproductive specialists, make sure to ask how they report the stats to SART and the CDC. If they report them as a whole, then you need to ask what your particular doctor's success rates have been over the course of the last year.

Additionally, statistics on multiple births are also reported to SART. If a clinic has a particularly high twin or triplet rate, then it is likely they are aggressive in their embryo transfer protocols to maintain high pregnancy statistics. This type of transfer method, unfortunately, leads to a greater number of selective reduction cases and high-risk pregnancies. It's something to definitely inquire about as you narrow down your list of prospective clinics.

TECHNICAL CONSIDERATIONS FOR YOUR EGG DONOR CYCLE

Aside from the office demeanor and statistical considerations for clinic selection, how do you move forward with your choice given all of the technologies available to today's fertility patients? We'll give you a review of the most common technologies and related considerations that might affect your decisions.

Preimplantation Genetic Diagnosis

Preimplantation genetic diagnosis (PGD) refers to a newer series of diagnostic procedures performed on embryos prior to implantation. PGD offers a way to do embryo screening that tests for chromosomal abnormalities. High-risk patients are therefore often very interested in this particular genetic screening technology. High risk could mean the mother or egg donor is of advanced maternal age (older than 35), or someone with a family history of a genetic disorder that could potentially affect their offspring. PGD testing can also determine the sex of the embryo with a nearly 100% accuracy rate (www.genderselectioncenter.com/treatments/pgd).

In general, PGD is performed for one of two reasons:

- Known or possible genetic disorder or
- Sex selection

The use of PGD varies vastly from clinic to clinic and is a continued source of debate. Most doctors feel very strongly that the only valid reason to perform PGD is to determine the health of the embryos in high-risk situations. Thus, if you choose a healthy, young egg donor who passes her genetic evaluation and required genetic testing, there would be no medical reason for performing PGD on the embryos (assuming the sperm donor is also clear of genetic disorders). One study stated a nearly 40% error rate where PGD testing made it appear as if the tested embryos showed abnormal or missing chromosomes, when in fact the embryos were actually healthy.[9]

There are many reasons that people may choose to sex select. However, if there is no other medical necessity for PGD, it is prudent to consider that there could be a high percentage of good embryos lost along with the embryos of the undesired sex should you choose to rely on the results of this testing method 100%. This means there is the potential of ending up with few or no embryos or only enough to do a fresh cycle transfer and nothing leftover to freeze. Ultimately, you might be put in the situation of deciding whether you want to be a parent or a parent to only one sex.

If you are using PGD for anything other than a known or high-risk genetic disorder, make sure that you ask the following questions:

- What is your success rate on donor egg-transferred PGD embryos? Is it higher, the same, or lower?
- How many embryos are typically left over to freeze after PGD has been performed?
- What is the cost of PGD at their clinic? Costs typically vary from $4,000–$10,000.
- What are the stipulations for performing PGD? Will they allow sex selection or does the clinic only use PGD for genetic screening?
- How hard is PGD pushed for nonrisk embryos? There is no valid study showing a higher rate of pregnancy or lower rate of miscarriage on PGD performed on healthy embryos.

Blastocyst versus Three-Day Embryo Transfers

When it comes to your embryos, different clinics favor different growth stages for ideal transfers. The two most popular growth stages at which to perform a transfer are stages blastocyst and three-day embryo, both of which have their risks and advantages. A blastocyst is an embryo that has undergone multiple cellular divisions with the formation of a cavity within it. A fertilized egg reaches the blastocyst stage usually five or six days after fertilization. It is believed that a blastocyst has a better chance of implanting not just because it has shown a competency to develop further, but also because of some further maturation of surface receptors that might increase the chance of attachment to the endometrium.

One of the benefits of a blastocyst-stage transfer is the statistically higher chance of survival. This translates to lower risk procedures than those where multiple embryos are transferred in the hopes that one will carry to term and a decreased chance of multiples pregnancy, which is always a higher risk scenario. Ultimately, this means there are fewer cases of selective reduction or high-risk multiple pregnancies when using a blast embryo.

The potential disadvantage in using blastocyst is that an embryo, which does not make it to the blast stage, would not have made it in the uterus either. The problem is, this isn't definite. If you choose to take your full cycle of embryos to the blast stage and only one or two survive, there would be little chance of having any embryos left for a future frozen cycle should you want a second child or in the event of a miscarriage or failed transfer.

In speaking with several different doctors who have used both three-day and blastocyst embryo transfer methods, the consistent consensus is that success rates continue to be 30% to 50% higher with blastocyst embryos. However, if there is a limited number of embryos to work with following the retrieval process, three-day is generally preferred as there is no added benefit to waiting.

Intracytoplasmic Sperm Injection

Intracytoplasmic sperm injection (ICSI) is a technique whereby a single sperm is manually injected into an egg by an embryologist in the laboratory. It is performed when there is a very low sperm count or when the sperm shows poor motility. It is also indicated when there is poor fertilization of eggs in a previous IVF cycle. The procedure involves grasping a single sperm with a very fine needlepoint pipette and then gently inserting it inside the egg and releasing the sperm. ICSI is also indicated when frozen sperm is to be used. ICSI improves fertilization rate and might yield better quality embryos.

Assisted Hatching

The most common reasons why an IVF cycle may not succeed are

- the embryo does not implant into the uterus or
- the embryo does not hatch.

Assisted hatching (AH) is a method used to help the egg implant into the uterus with a higher level of success. The layers of proteins that protect the embryo until it reaches the blastocyst stage are called the *zona pellicuda*. In AH, a hole is poked in the *zona* to help the embryo better implant in the uterus. This method is typically only used for women of advanced maternal age or multiple failed IVF cycles. It's important to discuss the need for AH for a donor egg embryo; however, if you don't have a uterine lining factor, the embryos created from donor eggs might render this technology unnecessary. You'll also want to inquire about the clinic's embryologist(s) and their experience with AH. This procedure is considered relatively risk free so long as the embryologist performing the procedure has the commensurate experience.

Vitrification

Vitrification is a technology that allows for the rapid freezing of unfertilized eggs from a retrieval procedure. Older slow-freezing methods have been shown to cause ice crystals to form on the eggs, which could cause damage to the cell structure. This is still considered an experimental technology in assisted reproduction, so be sure to ask a lot of questions if you are planning to freeze or have been recommended by your fertility specialist to freeze your unfertilized eggs via the vitrification.

HOW DOES YOUR DOCTOR'S OFFICE COME ACROSS IN THE PRESS?

The fertility industry tends to keep a relatively low profile in the press, but when we make the headlines, it's not without a sensationalized splash. From octomom to mixed-up or lost embryos, there's nothing more heartbreaking for us than to see a fertility clinic make the headlines in all of the wrong ways. So how do they perform under scrutiny if such cases have arisen with the clinic and, contrarily, how are they presented in the media and other outlets such as online support groups?

Most clinics have a press page on their Web site where you can review notable news coverage the clinic has received. It's also a great place for you to launch your own web search, which can unearth sentiment about a particular clinic or physician that their Web site won't share with you. If you come across a clinic and/or a doctor who comes up over and over again as being unethical, displaying poor bedside manner, aggressive, and so forth, then it is very important to take this into consideration. There are numerous wonderful reproductive endocrinologists and clinics alike out there who have your best interests at heart and act in an honest, straightforward manner.

It's always important to remember that the press doesn't get everything right all the time, and there are always two sides to every story. Take all of the information you find with a grain of salt, but take note of repeated negative experiences and ultimately, trust your gut instincts.

CONSISTENCY WITHIN A CLINIC

If you're going to partner with a clinic to build your family, it's important to know that you're going to be able to build relationships with the people dedicated to helping achieve your dreams. Although any place of business experiences staff coming and going, it's likely you want to work with a clinic that shows excellent retention rates and long-term tenures with both their staff and physicians. There's no shame in asking about turnover rates or the average tenure for both staff and physicians at a clinic. As with any business, people sometimes move on to different opportunities for varying reasons, but if there has been a consistently high turnover of both staff and doctors over the last several years, that could possibly be a red flag as to the internal culture of that particular facility.

AGE RESTRICTIONS

Although it might not be something you've considered, most fertility clinics do establish age restrictions on patients they are willing to treat. The age guideline with which most clinics works is they prefer the intended parents' ages not to exceed 110 years when added together. For single female intended parents, Wendie's experience has shown a trend of restricting embryo implantation in women exceeding ages 50–55. We've seen exceptions made to this age range for intended mothers who will be using a gestational surrogate, however, and although there are clinics that operate outside of these guidelines, they are more difficult to find.

There are many ethical considerations that fertility clinics consistently face, and age for intended mothers is one of them. Vicken Sahakian, MD, of Pacific Fertility Center in Los Angeles (who has also generously lent his insights to this book) had a case where an intended mother falsified her patient records to show her age as 10 years younger than she truly was. The result was that she became one of the oldest women to become pregnant via IVF and gave birth to twins at the age of 66. She was a single mother and passed away at age 69 when the twins were only two years old.

As there is no exact science as to how long parents will live, what their health will be like in the future, or how able-bodied they might be to raise young, energetic children, we're sure you can understand how age for intended parents is a weighty issue for IVF clinics. A multitude of factors often go into making the decision to work with an older parent, such as health of the intended parents, health of the mother carrying the child, who will raise the children should something happen to the parents, and how solid is the social support system of the parents as a whole. Our ethical obligation rest in making the best decision possible for not only the intended parents but also for any children we help to bring into the world through our services and efforts.

DECISION-MAKING FLEXIBILITY AND DOCTOR CLARITY

Although there are some intended parents who prefer to entrust the entire process from donor selection to treatment decisions to their IVF clinic and egg donor agency, it's much more the norm to encounter those who prefer to be an active part of the process. There are so many decisions to make, we find that intended parents who are active participants tend to be happier with processes as a whole—after all, it's your family you're taking a role in creating. For example, you should have a final say as to how many embryos are transferred, whether PGD is performed and if ICSI is used. There are some clinics that require any unused embryos be either (a) donated to their research center or (b) donated to another couple. Be sure to understand your choice of clinic's policy on untransferred embryos and unfertilized eggs.

Additionally, your doctor's office should also support the egg donor you want to use. It is a doctor's responsibility to tell you if they do not feel she would be a good candidate for you from a medical perspective, but beyond that, it is *your* decision. There are always going to be offices that, for simplicity's sake, present the best-case scenario for a donor choice. For example, some offices will suggest that you use a local donor to make help control costs, as well as give them the ability to directly monitor your donor throughout her cycle. Although practicality shouldn't be ignored, your clinic should always keep in mind that this is your cycle and future child. If you want to work with a donor who lives in a different state or city, then you should be the one who ultimately determines if the additional cost is worth it.

Another example of clinics opting for simplicity is with in-house donor pools. Some clinics have a small database of in-house donors and will only allow their intended parents to select from their pool. This can be problematic if you are seeking a more difficult-to-find donor and only have 20 donors to choose from. Also, some clinics with in-house donors will allow you to choose donors from outside agencies; however, their fees jump up significantly if you do. Unless your clinic's donors are prescreened genetically, psychologically, and medically before they are matched with intended parents, the cost difference to use a donor either in-house or through an agency should be minimal to none. As you interview prospective clinics, be sure to inquire about whether or not they have an in-house donor pool and what their policies are on accepting donors from outside agencies should you choose to do so.

To make all of the best decisions for you and your family, you also need to feel as if they're giving you the best service possible and available at reasonable intervals. Are you able to get someone on the phone when you call? Are you clear about the process or are you being talked to as though you wouldn't understand, so why bother explaining? Do you get things explained to you just hours before you have to make the decision, or were all common scenarios discussed ahead of time so you could take the appropriate time to weigh your options?

Here is an experience shared by one of Wendie's intended fathers. He started with one IVF clinic and finished with another due to the challenges he encountered along the way. Although we always hope for a positive relationship for all intended parents and their clinics of choice, we hope his insights will help you avoid a similar situation with your IVF clinic:

> It is assumed that the medical community is knowledgeable, but communication skills are not a job requirement for them. And it is so frustrating when doctors, nurses, and staff blurt out a fusillade of medical jargon as if you've gone through medical school. It's more than presumptuous; it's lazy and negligent. They were always so busy, we felt like we were becoming the "high maintenance" client if we asked them to explain something again. They exhibited blatant impatience if I ask a question. First and foremost, assuming it's important to be informed when you make a decision, it's so easy to just throw up your hands and say you'll do whatever the doctor recommends. And when the doctor says it's your choice, it sometimes comes to the point that you're reduced metaphorically to "closing your eyes and dropping your finger on your selection." Not good. Furthermore, when you don't know what's going on, it amps up the stress. You know how it is; fear of the unknown. Helplessness.

Sure, you can Google the issues at hand and that helps to a point. But you absolutely need to talk to somebody who can answer your questions in the terms and scenarios that you are facing at the time, which oftentimes are unique and not readily addressed on Internet research sources or chat rooms.

When it comes time to embark on such an important journey in your life, remember that comfort and understanding about the process and all of the decisions being made throughout should be just as much a priority for your chosen IVF clinic as they are to you.

HOW MANY CYCLES DOES YOUR CLINIC PERFORM PER YEAR?

It is considered an accepted rule in our industry that a clinic should perform at least 60–100 cycles per year, with 20% being donor egg. The reason for this is that you want to be sure that they are doing enough cycles to provide accurate data for their clinic statistics and not skewing it with a few exceptional (or unexceptional) results. You also want to be sure that you are not working with a clinic that is using you as a "practice" patient on how to do an egg donation cycle. If a clinic is asking either you or your agency how to perform a cycle, then it's time to move along. It does happen, and Wendie's agency has been contacted by a clinic to find out what the required FDA tests were for egg donors and also asked if the agency could teach the donor how to administer her injections.

Although you want your IVF clinic to be well practiced in the realms of both IVF and egg donation, you should also take the time to determine if one of the clinics you're considering is, perhaps, *too* busy. If a clinic is doing an exceedingly high number of cycles per month, will you still get the personal attention that you need and deserve? Will you go through the cycle feeling as though you have the doctor and nursing staff's attention enough to ask questions and get answers, or will you feel like just another person in the crowd being herded along? Will they allow you to have a cycle when it is convenient for you, or do they mandate your schedule based solely on the doctor's schedule? Do they perform retrievals at any time during the month, or do they schedule in a way that all retrievals are on the first week of every month, no exceptions?

Remember, every clinic won't be a perfect fit for you and your needs. Work with the clinic and professionals who make you feel comfortable throughout the process. Don't settle for second best when there are so many qualified and compassionate reproductive doctors available to help you along on your journey.

Shelly's Story—A Mother Via Shared Cycle

When we were doing the fertility dance, there were so many obstacles, not the least of which was cost. Early on, we opted for options that brought us little chance for success, purely because we were driven by price. It was just a year or two after 9/11, the economy was in the tank, I was in the throes of launching a startup, and we were getting by on one salary instead of two. Ergo, price drove decisions.

Once we finally realized that using an egg donor gave us the greatest chance of actually ever having a baby, we very quickly knew that the only way we could afford that option was via the shared cycle offered by our doctor. And today, in spite of anyone's financial circumstances, to my pragmatic self, it still seems like a terrific option. When you go down this path, you realize that parents are the people who raise a child, and you also realize that whose egg it is and/or how many other eggs there might be out there that originated from a single source are so insignificant.

The donor we used (I still bless her to this day) provided eggs to two other parents hoping for children at the same time she so generously donated to us. And those eggs weren't the finished product, but they allowed us to begin. My husband is what made those eggs into embryos, and then my womb is the place those embryos grew and thrived. And now, five years later, two little girls continue to light our lives on a daily basis.

One final point—you can never know what will happen to you during the course of that aforementioned fertility dance. In spite of the cost savings of a shared cycle egg donation, there are occasional obstacles. Along the way, due to rogue circumstances, we lost not one, but two separate sets of twins. So not only did that fertility dance take us three years, it ended up costing us in excess of $30,000—even when using the more cost-effective method of shared cycle egg donations.

SHARED CYCLES

A shared cycle is when a clinic is willing to work with one donor and split the eggs and cost between two sets of intended parents. Some offices willingly do shared cycles, especially with proven donors who have produced a high egg yield. Others refuse to do it at all for a few reasons. First, a shared cycle generally means less revenue for the doctor's office, as they are splitting the cost of everything. Second, there is always the risk that one parent will get pregnant whereas the other one does not. The questions could be posed that they didn't get the "better" quality eggs or that something went wrong with their embryos. The legal contract is also a consideration, as there will need to be an addendum regarding which parent gets the "extra" egg if the retrieval results in an odd number (i.e., if there are 21 eggs at retrieval, one parent will get 10 eggs and the other, 11).

If your doctor's office does participate in shared cycles and this is an option you would like to consider to save costs, we've put together a list of pros and cons to consider and discuss with your clinic.

Pros

- More cost-efficient (split: donor fee, medications, and monitoring)
- Almost always a previous, proven donor (most agencies or clinics would not risk a shared cycle with a first-time donor)
- Less chance of having excessive leftover embryos
- Donor with historically high egg production

Cons

- Fewer eggs available for fertilization per recipient
- Must decide who gets the extra egg if the cycle produces an odd number of eggs
- Risk of having no embryos to freeze
- Must coordinate cycles among three people instead of two
- Donor may undergo a more aggressive stimulation cycle to produce a larger number of viable eggs

COST

This may seem like an odd topic to address given that all clinics will ultimately share their fees with you, whether early in the interview process or after you've said you'd like to proceed. However, we wanted to address this issue as there have been countless stories over the years of intended parents who have shared fees that have been nearly triple the average industry rates. No one should be taken advantage of, and we'll explore the average range of IVF with donor egg cycle fees so you have the most current information to assist in your decision making.

Most clinics are at least within the same ballpark, give or take a few thousand dollars. For example, an egg donation cycle using an egg donor and the intended mother as the gestational carrier will always be around $15,000, give or take a couple thousand. Although there are other things that could cause this fee to increase (such as PGD, ICSI, sperm spinning, embryo freezing, additional medications, etc.), it's a solid base number from which to work.

Some clinics also offer something called "shared risk" programs where you pay a higher premium to start the process, but if it doesn't work, you get a second cycle for virtually no cost. The advantages for shared risk programs are

- Your doctor is extremely motivated for you to get pregnant on the initial fresh cycle transfer
- Should something go wrong or you don't get pregnant, your next cycle is covered

Disadvantages

- Higher initial cost
- When/if you do get pregnant with the fresh cycle transfer, you will receive no refund regardless of the cost of the shared risk program

IN CLOSING

Choosing a clinic has numerous facets, and our goal was to give you as many of those to consider as possible as you embark on the process. As geography is the least of your concerns, you should have a solid information set to start narrowing down what are the most important qualities of your potential partners on the medical side of your journey toward family. Not every office offers the same options, has the same stats or is as experienced as others, and, ultimately, the best choice is the one that will make you feel at ease with moving forward. Although it may seem like you've waited a long time to get where you are, remember that taking just a little extra time to interview more than one doctor and/or clinic might be the difference between making this journey something worth taking versus heaping more heartache onto what's already shared its fair portion of stress.

The process can feel somewhat long, but just stick through it, one foot in front of the other. Take a breath, relax, and enjoy the journey; the journey is awesome (and this from a type A personality). I have met so many wonderful folks through this—not the least of which was my reproductive endocrinologist. He was the third doctor I interviewed, and from the time I walked in his door until the time I was told I was pregnant, I never once doubted he was the right fit for me. The amount of love that he and his staff showed me in this process has just opened up my heart even more.—*Anonymous recipient mother*

Key Chapter Highlights—How to Choose a Reproductive Clinic

- Approximately 600 IVF clinics in the United States, 441 of which reported their success rates to SART.

- Not all clinics report their statistics to SART.

- Be sure to review success rates directly with the clinic in relation to your scenario.

See Appendix A for a list of suggested interview questions for fertility clinics.

5

How to Choose an Egg Donor Agency

When you've reached a certain point, you'll need to select an egg donor agency to help you continue your journey. Although some reproductive clinics offer in-house egg donor matching services, the most common way recipient parents locate their donors is through a third-party agency. Whether in-house or third party, this will be your team that will handle the legwork involved in coordinating your donor and helping you travel with her throughout the process until the retrieval (when her eggs are harvested and prepared for fertilization in the IVF lab). Throughout the years, we've heard countless times that there isn't a definitive checklist for what recipient parents should look for and criteria for evaluating an egg donor agency. We hope that, with the information that follows, we've filled that gap and will give you a solid list of resources that will help you

- research egg donor agencies by geography, technology, reputation, and results

- ask the right questions of prospective agencies so you understand fully everyone's role in your journey

- perform your own research and be comfortable with the information you receive, which can only make your decision to select a certain agency be more comfortable

We won't say we're not biased about best practices because we strive to achieve those each day with our clients. However, we'll show you both sides of the coin, so you can make the best possible decisions for you and your family. After all—we're all hoping for the same outcome, a family.

A WORD ON "BAD AGENCIES"

With the number of years we've been in the fertility and egg donation industry, it's inevitable that not every egg donor cycle or eventual transfer turns out

47

the way we would have hoped. No matter where things got bogged down along the way, we don't want to spend time belaboring the issue that sometimes things just don't work out. What we think is most important is that you go into this process with eyes wide open, knowing that sometimes, no matter how hard your agency is working for you, challenges might present themselves. The cycle didn't work, the donor backed out, your donor may even discover something about her health history through genetic testing that she had no way of knowing. There are any number of reasons egg donor cycles don't proceed as planned. It has happened before, and it's our hope that it doesn't happen to you. However, if you see yourself facing these challenges, know that there are countless families who have overcome these obstacles and gone through subsequent cycles to build their family.

RESEARCHING AGENCIES: INSIGHT FROM INDUSTRY AUTHORITIES

Our goal is to help you find out what questions to ask, where to find out if it's a reputable agency, and also to make sure that you find the right agency for your personal needs. As Wendie owns a full-service egg donation agency, we felt it wouldn't be fair to you if we only shared her thoughts on what you should look for in an agency. So, as a way to avoid bias and provide you with the best information possible, there was no better person for us to approach to share her thoughts on researching egg donor agencies than Marna Gatlin, the founder of Parents Via Egg Donation (PVED).

PVED is one of the fastest growing nonprofit educational and support organizations dedicated to working directly with those researching and going through the egg donation process. Marna is also the mother of an incredible little boy who was conceived through egg donation, and he's the reason behind her passion and years of endless effort poured into this nonprofit program.

What follows is in Marna's words and offers perhaps the most comprehensive list of what you should be looking for and evaluating in your search for the right egg donation agency. And by "right," we mean right for you. There are so many moving parts in play, from the emotional side like personalities and donor rosters to the statistical and financial aspects, that only you will know when you've found the right match. The information that follows, however, will give you the best foundation possible from which to begin your evaluation process.

What I have found throughout the years is that egg donor agencies come in all shapes and sizes. Some egg donor agencies are large and well established, while others are small and brand new to the third-party industry. What I tell every intended parent that contacts PVED is that regardless of which egg donor agency you select, we want every intended parent to be educated and informed as they go through the process. Above all, egg donor agencies are service providers, meaning they work for *you*. You are in the driver's seat. While they may have the egg donor you want to grow your family, you are writing that check and they need *your* business to stay in business.

When researching an egg donor agency, the simplest thing to do is to call them. Talk to someone at the agency, and get a feel for the way they do business. Was the person answering the phone genuinely interested in speaking with you? Did you connect with a live person? Do they return calls promptly? If you contacted the agency by e-mail, did they reply in a timely manner? If your answer is "no" to any of the questions, I'd recommend continuing your search with other agencies as once you are a client, their communication with you as an intended parent isn't going to be much better.

Your physician and donor coordinator are also a great resource when selecting an egg donor agency. Your clinic will be able to share with you their experience in working with various agencies with regards to communication, quality of egg donors, and how they conduct their business.

"I asked some friends what agencies they used. In one case I couldn't find any donors I liked, in another I had heard mixed things about the agency from people in my online support group. So many times throughout my donation process I went to the boards to ask questions—about agencies, doctors, you name it. I found that a lifesaver." —*Anonymous intended mother using PVED.org*

Those you meet online on bulletin boards, chat rooms, and forums specifically focused on egg donation and third-party reproduction are an often overlooked source for referrals to agencies. There is no better advertising than word of mouth. Speak to other parents who have had children via egg donation and listen to their experiences. They'll be more than happy to share their trials and tribulations as well as glowing reviews for the people who helped them become a family. At Parents Via Egg Donation (www.pved.org), we've built a community that allows us to connect intended parents and those who have achieved parenthood through egg donation. Our forums are incredible sources for firsthand information, and we also provide information on agencies, reproductive clinics, reproductive attorneys, and egg donor experiences as well. We are a nonprofit, and our mission is to help you have the best possible experience on your path to building your family.

The authors, Wendie and Erika, asked me to compile a list of questions readers of this book could use as they begin researching egg donor agencies. While what follows isn't exhaustive, it should give you a good starting point, and perhaps make you think of a few questions you might not have thought to ask.

1. How long have you been in business and/or working in this field?

2. How many donors has your agency matched with recipients in the last year?

3. Do you have references from clinics and previous client/parents?

4. How many donors do you have available in your agency?

5. What is the agency's refund policy?

6. What are your agency's fees, and what exactly do they cover?

7. Does your agency provide a service agreement between the egg donor agency and the intended parent?

8. How much is your typical donor compensation, and when/how is that compensation given to the donor?

9. Do you allow your donors to set their own level of compensation?

10. Does your agency require egg donors to undergo psychological screening before being placed on the prospective donor list or after they have been chosen? Who performs the screening? (i.e., the agency or a third-party psychological professional)

11. If we were to desire an open egg donation, will your agency facilitate a meeting between us and the egg donor?

12. Does your agency facilitate anonymous, open, or both kinds of egg donations?

13. How does your egg donor agency manage its information and records regarding its donors?

14. Where does your agency keep this information?

15. How long will the agency keep this information? If for instance the agency goes out of business, who would be responsible for keeping information on past clients, previous cycles, and egg donors in case a need were to arise to contact an egg donor?

16. Does the agency adhere to the American Society for Reproductive Medicine guidelines for egg donation?

17. What kind of medical insurance coverage for the egg donor does your agency provide, and what are the terms? Are these costs included in our fees to the agency or paid separately to the insurance company?

18. Who provides the legal contract between the intended parent and the egg donor? Do we need to secure our own reproductive attorney?

19. How are recipient parents protected in the event the egg donor chooses to discontinue the process halfway through a cycle? How is the recipient parent protected in the event the egg donor doesn't take her medication as agreed?

20. Does your agency's fees change depending on our method of payment (e.g., cash, credit card, wire transfer, check)?

21. What are the typical donor fee ranges? What causes one donor's fee to be higher than another's?

22. Does your agency provide an itemized list of expenses?

23. What can we expect with regard to contact with the agency during the cycle?

We've also included this information in Appendix B for your convenience.

INSIDE THE QUESTIONS

We know Marna's list could be seen as daunting. Some of those questions might not even apply to your personal scenario. We'll do our best to further explore some of these questions and why they're worth asking of any egg donor agency your might consider.

How Long Has the Agency Been in Business?

Given the growth of the third-party reproductive industry in the past decade, egg donor agencies are cropping up all over the United States, and it's good to know how long the agency has been in business. Some agencies are huge and have upwards of 3,000 egg donors on their sites. Others are small and like to run their agencies more like a boutique—choosing to be highly selective thus keeping available donors numbers low. The most important thing to keep in mind, however, is that agency longevity doesn't necessarily mean better, nor does a newer agency mean less qualified or competent.

If you're considering a newer agency, find out how long the owners and the principals have been in the reproductive and egg donation industry and what their job was prior to owning their own agency. If an agency was started by an egg donor whose only experience in the industry is that she has donated a few times, that's different than someone who has years of experience working directly with intended parents either for a different agency or a medical facility. A more important question to ask is how many cycles has the staff coordinated during their tenure in this industry? For example, a new agency with a staff that has collectively coordinated more than a thousand cycles is significantly more experienced than a new agency with a staff that has coordinated 20.

If you're working with an agency that's been around for a while, what do the discussion boards say about the agency and its owners? Do they have a good reputation and are they well liked by the industry as a whole? Does your IVF clinic know the agency? What has been their experience in coordinating cycles with the agency? Because IVF clinics are particular regarding the egg donor agencies they work with, it's important that you listen and pay attention to the information they share with you about any specific egg donation agency. You'll find that IVF clinics are incredibly candid about the egg donation agencies with which they've worked. If your IVF clinic likes an agency and goes on to say positive things about them, it's much more likely that communication will flow more smoothly through your donor cycle, which isn't something to be taken lightly.

How Many Cycles Did the Agency Coordinate Last Year? How Many Got Canceled and Why?

To be safe, we'd say that you should hold your egg donation agency to the same statistical standard as your IVF clinic. A minimum of 60 cycles per year would be a safe number for reputable programs, which is roughly five to six cycles per month.

Although all programs will have some donors who don't pass their medical or genetic screenings for reasons that no one could have anticipated, you want to be wary of programs who don't prescreen donors at all. If the agency director is telling you that a high percentage of their donors don't pass their screenings, then there might be an issue with their prescreening process.

It stands to reason that there should be a conversation with all donors about their personal lifestyle. Although these are young women, many of whom are not married and live a single life, you still don't want to risk working with someone who is with multiple sexual partners or doesn't practice safe sex. If you receive a donor profile for review where the donor indicates that she has had multiple sex partners in the past six months, caution should be taken as the risk of her contracting a sexually transmitted disease (STD) would be statistically higher. It's not a reason to entirely rule out a donor; as we know, life can change on a dime, but you're entrusting this donor with your cycle. There should also be a verbal conversation followed by a signed statement that they understand that they will be tested for both recreational and prescription drugs. Furthermore, your agency should have in writing and a verbal confirmation from all donors that they would pass their drug, alcohol, and, to the best of their knowledge, the STD testing. From a realistic standpoint, agencies aren't only looking for donors who are not sexually active or who never have the occasional glass of wine with dinner, as that is neither practical nor necessary. Rather, we're looking for donors with lifestyles that are more conducive for ensuring they will pass their initial screenings to the best of our knowledge.

Agencies can't control every unknown medical situation any more than most donors can. However, they are able to prescreen in such ways as to troubleshoot some of the situations that might arise. Ultimately, an agency is only able to pass along the information that the egg donors share with them. With that knowledge, you should be able to ask an agency director how many cycles they do per year and how many of these actually make it through to completion.

Do You Have References from Other Intended Parents and Clinics?

It is a given in the egg donation industry that many people who are going through assisted reproduction feel as though it is a very private and/or personal journey. However, all agencies will have a handful of parents who are not only enthusiastic about their experiences, but also willing to talk to others who are going through the process. If you're feeling as though you would like to reach out to someone else who has gone through a cycle with the agency you have chosen, they should be able to set you up with some recipient parents with whom you can have a candid conversation.

Perhaps even more important than this, all reputable agencies will have a list of IVF clinics and doctors they have worked with over the years who are happy to give you a reference. It doesn't necessarily need to be your doctor, rather it could be other clinics you could call and ask them about their experiences with your prospective agency of choice. There are reasons that IVF clinics choose to work with certain agencies over others, and so there is no better reference than a clinic who feels an agency provides quality donors, exceptional service to their intended parents, and bundles all of that together with ethical business practices. IVF clinics would hurt their own reputation if they chose to continuously work with agencies whose practices and donors didn't result in rewarding experiences.

Another place to look for references would be the online community. As Marna mentioned, there are many online resources and discussion boards where recipient parents and other intended parents talk openly about their experiences with different agencies. It's a great way to see which agencies continue to shine with people just like you. It's also a good place to get inside information on what to expect if you work with a specific agency, such as the types of contracts they use, donor quality, type of service you can expect, and more. There's really no better way to be prepared for an egg donor agency experience than hearing the thoughts and experiences of those who have come before you.

How Many Donors Do You Have Available in Your Agency?

Egg donor agency rosters vary from as few as 20 donors up to as high as 3,000; however, most of them fall somewhere in the 200–600 category. The issue that comes up when working with an agency with a smaller donor pool is that your options are limited and there may not be a donor with whom you can connect. On the other hand, they probably know their donors or at least can share some insight with you into each one's personality, as there aren't so many that the ladies get lost in the crowd. An agency with 1,000 or more donors is likely not going to know or remember most of the donors they interviewed and brought into the program, so there is less of a chance to get personal insight into the type of person your chosen donor might be beyond her donor application. Obviously, this is not the case with all agencies, whether large or small. It's more what we typically hear from many of the intended parents we've worked with throughout the years who have experienced both sides of the spectrum.

What Is the Agency's Refund Policy?

Agency refund policies are as diverse as the donors they have on their rosters. What you should know as you begin to evaluate prospective agencies is that there's a reason they've built their refund policy the way they have, and it's one that works best for their practice. What you can decide is which one works best for you. We'll discuss the four most common refund policies so that when you choose your agency, you can be aware and prepared for what occurs should the cycle be canceled or modified for any reason.

No Refund Policy

Once you choose a donor, confirm her and sign the contract—your money belongs to the agency. If she doesn't pass her psychological, genetic, or medical screening, or otherwise cannot or chooses not to move forward, or you chose not to move forward, your money will not be refunded. You will, in *most* cases, be able to choose a different donor with their agency at no additional program fee.

Nonrefundable Down Payment

Upon selection of a donor, the agency will require a nonrefundable down payment that is retained regardless of whether a donor passes any of her initial screenings or any of the parties back out. I've seen this fee as low as $500 and as high as up to half the program fee. This usually means that you can have the remainder of the funds sent back to you or you can select a new donor but must replenish the nonrefundable fee.

Selective Nonrefundable Fee

The full program fee is retained only if your donor passes her genetic, psychological, and initial medical screening. If for any reason your donors starts her medication but is unable to complete the cycle, the program fee is still retained. There is usually a reduced program fee if you want to start again either with the same donor or a different donor.

Earned Program Fee

The program fee is broken down into segments based on what the agency feels they have earned. For example, they retain "x" amount of their program fee after a donor passes genetic and psychological evaluations. They earn another portion after she passes medical screening and so on throughout the cycle.

What's most important to find out from your agency is what happens if your cycle is canceled for any reason. There will almost always be a policy in place and some are stricter than others. Also ask what happens if a cycle doesn't result in a pregnancy and you decide to do a second cycle. Will the agency offer a reduced cycle fee regardless of which donor you choose? Is this fee applied equally to both the same and a new donor? How much is this discount?

Remember: egg donation agencies cannot work for free, nor would they survive if they did. What they can do is have a very clear and concisely written contract that states exactly where your money is going and when and what the circumstances are in which they will retain the fees.

What Are the Agency Fees and What Do They Cover?

We can only speak to what our experience has been regarding program fees, but we'll give you ranges that are average across the industry to help guide you. On average, agency fees fall somewhere between $4,000 and $8,000 per donor cycle. Factors contributing to the range can be geographic location of the agency, longevity, and also what the fee covers (as it varies drastically from agency to agency). You might find an agency that charges fees that are higher or lower than the range discussed here, but it's often a factor of how they break down their fee structures.

Some charge a flat fee that will completely cover the overhead for your cycle. The most common inclusions in an agency's program fees are

- legal fees for you and your donor
- accident insurance policy for your donor (required by all IVF clinics and agencies)
- psychological and genetic evaluations for your donor
- matching and co-coordinating the cycle between your IVF clinic and egg donor
- escrow fees for donor compensation funds

So you may be charged somewhere in between $6,000 and $8,000 to cover all of the agency's program fees.

Other agencies break it down into separate accounts: fees that you owe the agency directly and fees owed to outside vendors. For example, the program fee may be anywhere from $4,000–$7,000 and that is paid directly to the agency for their coordination of your cycle. The fees for attorneys, geneticist, psychologist, insurance company, and others may then be an additional cost, which are paid into a separate escrow account.

It is very important to find out exactly what your agency fee covers, so here are examples of the additional fees that could be incurred if not included in your program fee:

- Recipient parent attorney fees: $550–$2,500
- Accident insurance policy: $245–$500
- Genetic evaluation: $150–$350
- Psychological evaluation: $125–$500
- Donor and recipient background check: $25–$100
- Donor travel expenses: $200–$4,000
- Escrow fees: $150–$750
- Egg donor incidentals: $50–$500 (birth control pill, parking, vitamins, extra medication, reimbursement, etc.)

Note that egg donor agencies are not required to use an escrow service to handle certain fees. However, if an agency does not use a separate, independent escrow company, make sure that they have a superior reputation within the industry. Ask your doctor's office if they've heard of any issues with that particular program. Check the discussion boards and online support groups. You may also ask if your agency is willing to hold all fees that do not go directly to the agency within a licensed escrow account. There are many to choose from, and most charge a nominal fee. Ask your egg donor agency for a list of escrow agencies with which they have established relationships. If they don't have a list to provide, ask your reproductive law attorney for his or her recommendations. Although most agencies are above board, there are some who have been known to mismanage funds. Using a separate escrow service is the best way to ensure that your accounts are being handled with the utmost honesty.

Also, find out if your agency has one program fee or whether it varies based on the donor you choose. Some programs charge a higher program fee if you use a donor who is considered to have more desirable attributes, such as previous pregnancy successes and/or high egg count, specific look, education, profession, or athletic ability.

Ask your agency if they take a percentage of the donor's fee or whether she receives the entirety. This means that if the donor fee is $8,000, the agency can take 10% or $800 (in addition to the program fee they have already charged you). This could possibly encourage an agency to drive up the donor fees so that they get a higher percentage off the top of her fee. After all, 10% of $10,000 is better than 10% of $8,000 from a financial standpoint.

When agencies are dealing with people's emotions, future, finances, lives, dream, and so forth—there is a huge responsibility for professionals to operate with empathy. There are even some agencies who will offer discounts if you select a first-time donor. This is always a good question to ask because it is to the benefit of any agency to have repeat donors on their database. Most agencies expect their donors to take a lower fee for their first cycle (industry standard fees for first-time donors are almost always $5,000–$6,000, regardless of their attributes). It's sort of a "good faith" agreement between the donor and the agency that they will not charge as much, she will not charge as much; and in future cycles, donor fees can be renegotiated if there is a positive outcome. This is not the case for all agencies any more than it's the case that all donors take a lower first-time fee, but you should be aware that it is common enough that it's worth mentioning. And although there are agencies that discount certain fees when using first-time donors, that's not an indication of whether the agency is reputable or not—it's just a matter of varying business practices. Nonetheless, it never hurts to ask in cases where there *might* be financial flexibility as you start on this journey.

Does the Agency Provide a Service Agreement between the Egg Donor Agency and Intended Parent?

Every egg donation agency should have a service agreement between themselves and their intended parents. Typically, these agreements cover

- the agency's scope and duties
- what your fees pay for and how they are held

57

- cancellation, failed and repeat cycle policies
- what the agency agrees to charge for subsequent cycles
- what the agency's responsibility is regarding your privacy
- what additional fees might be incurred in the case of noninsurance-covered emergencies with your egg donor during the course of the cycle
- arbitration of claims
- limitations of liability and what your recompense would be should the agency breech confidence or practice gross negligence in any way (ranges between $4,000 and $10,000)
- termination of agreement policies
- governing laws (if applicable)

Every agency agreement varies to some degree based on both circumstances they've encountered and their attorney's suggestion. Some agencies are known for their flexibility within the contract, whereas others are very rigid. Most agencies will allow changes for clarification or special circumstances specific to your cycle.

It's also important to recognize that agency agreements are drawn up for two very specific purposes above all others: first, is to define the program's policies and be sure that you agree to them, and second, to protect the agency. Agencies are essentially facilitators between all of the different entities that come together to make a cycle successful. So while an agency is responsible for making sure they follow through on all of their contracted responsibilities, they cannot be held responsible for the outcomes, information, or actions of all the different independent contractors who make an egg donor cycle a reality.

How Much Is the Typical Donor Compensation and When Is That Compensation Given to the Donor?

The question of donor compensation is one that will exist in the egg donation industry as long as the industry exists and also the area in which we see the most public debate about the industry as whole. As discussed previously in Chapter 3 regarding ASRM guidelines, that organization's suggested cap on egg donor compensation is $10,000. Most agencies comply (or at least strive to comply) with these guidelines, occasionally allowing for exceptions because of special circumstances. However, there are some agencies who do not feel it's necessary to limit donor compensation and will pay donors well above the suggested ASRM $10,000 cap.

Some agencies start all first-time donors at a preset compensation. Therefore, all first-time donor fees at that agency would be (for example) $6,000. For each subsequent cycle, the donor would receive an additional $1,500. This is just one example, as first-time and subsequent cycle fees vary from agency to agency.

Other agencies have a suggested first-time donor compensation fee but ultimately allow the egg donors themselves to determine what fee they would be comfortable with to move forward with the process. What we've found is that if a donor requests a fee that is extremely high without having a previous successful cycle on her record, it's difficult for her to get matched. Intended parents are rarely willing to risk that amount of money on an unproven donor. Therefore, it's much easier for agencies to suggest that first-time donors accept a lower fee that more intended parents can afford, and the agency can renegotiate her fee in the future as her cycle experience and performance might indicate.

The regulation of donor fees continues to be the subject of many debates. There is currently a class action lawsuit against several egg donation agencies along with ASRM and SART regarding teaming up together to price-fix egg donor compensation. In order for egg donation agencies to be an active member of either SART or ASRM, they are asked to sign something stating their compliance with the board of ethics guidelines regarding donor compensation. Thus, it was inevitable for many agencies that wanted to be a part of these institutions to agree to adhere to the guidelines and then stick with them to remain active members.

As we are both previous, repeat egg donors, an agency owner and friend, confidant, and guide to the many intended parents we have helped over the years, we understand both sides of the donor compensation debate.

When it comes to deciding on a donor, the process for which we'll cover in more detail in the next chapter, understand that there are thousands of women who are willing to share their genetic gift with you. No matter what your price threshold is, you'll find a wonderful young woman who will be a good match for you genetically and have the attributes you find most important. Higher fees aren't a guarantee of donor performance, but we'll help you understand the reasons in the following chapter as to why donor fees vary. Trust your instincts and the right donor will find her way to you!

Does Your Agency Require Donors to Undergo Psychological Screening before Being Placed on the Prospective Donor List? Who Performs the Screening (i.e., the Agency or a Third-Party Psychological Professional)?

The majority of egg donation agencies do in-house prescreening of prospective egg donors prior to admitting them into their program, albeit, not by a licensed psychological professional. These screenings typically include questions such as the following:

- Do you have family and/or friends who support your decision to be an egg donor?

- Are you able to take the time commitment to make all of your doctor's appointments?

- Are there any medical and/or psychological issues that would keep you from being able to follow through with the donation?

- Do you recognize that the intended parents are counting on you to be there to do everything that is required of you from the start of the cycle to the finish?

If a donor answers these questions and others during the prescreening process appropriately, they'll be placed on the roster of available donors and further psychological testing will be performed when they are matched with intended parents.

Some agencies have an in-house therapist or social worker on staff that prescreens all donors prior to being accepted into their agency. Most agencies, however, do not have a full psychological screening of a donor until she is officially chosen by an intended parent. This is because at any given time, over half of the donors in their program will never be matched with intended parents. Paying for a psychological evaluation, therefore, is typically considered the responsibility of the intended parent upon choosing an egg donor at the agency of their choice.

Once an egg donor is chosen, she would then be scheduled to have a psychological screening with a therapist or psychologist prior to her medical screening. Although some agencies and IVF clinics may not follow this exact order, this is what you will see the majority of the time. Standardized testing such as the Minnesota Multiphasic Personality Inventory (MMPI) or the NEO Personality Inventory are the most common types of screening. Others require an in-person psychological assessment only while others do an MMPI along with a follow-up in-person interview with the donor.

There is a strong case for all egg donors to do both the MMPI followed by an in-person evaluation. This will ensure both that the donor falls within the "normal" range of a written evaluation, and that she will also have the feedback from a professional who can speak to her about the questions she should consider as she embarks upon the donation process. If an egg donor passes both a written and in-person evaluation, it is a pretty safe bet that she will also be able to follow through with the demands of being an egg donor. We'll address this in more detail in Chapter 7.

If Desired, Would the Agency Facilitate a Meeting between the Intended Parent and the Egg Donor?

When we both began as donors in this industry, and subsequently, working as staff for egg donor agencies, it was rare that intended parents and egg donors chose to meet. At most, it seemed about 2%. Recently, it seems like that number has jumped up to 10%–15%. We feel that as the industry grows and more people start talking about this as an option to build their family, the taboo surrounding egg donation lightens, and the desire to meet the person who is helping you becomes stronger. The industry as a whole is starting to be more encouraging regarding the exchange of information and openness between intended parents and their egg donors. Whether it's for the sake of the children in the future or due to continued exchange regarding health history, the argument in favor of more open donations is being actively discussed and encouraged in third-party reproduction. There are certainly no expectations to meet your donor but there should be the option if this is what you would like to do.

The one standing rule that most agencies have is that in order for the intended parents and the egg donor to meet, both parties must agree to the meeting. Neither side should be forced into meeting if it's not in their comfort zone. If an intended parent wants to meet the donor they are interested in but she is not comfortable with it, they should consider working with a different donor, one more receptive to an open relationship.

Erika's Thoughts on Open Donations

I was an egg donor from 2002 to 2005, and until 2005 I'd never once met the recipient parents. For me, it wasn't necessary; and the people for whom I'd cycled were obviously okay with not meeting me as well. But in late 2004, there was a couple that wanted to meet me—I agreed without hesitation. From a donor's perspective, I can tell you that it was probably one of the coolest experiences in my life, to meet this couple and learn about them, their experiences and dreams. I was lucky enough to get a call the day their child was born and to this day, I still receive updates and visit with them when I happen to be on business in the city where they live. Open donations offer donors another level of fulfillment, and as my career's gone on to greater success, they've been with me on my journey as well. We're friendly, yet not friends—it's a beautiful way to peer through the looking glass into the life of another, knowing you each did something that made the other's life more fulfilling.

Many parents recently have broached the subject of not only meeting their donor, but also suggesting that she be open to future contact regarding medical issues, or if their children feel the need to meet or ask questions of their egg donor. This can be asked of the donor, but it's important to recognize that there is currently no legal obligation that can be enforced to make this an absolute. Even if your donor were to sign a legal contract stating that she is open to future contact, she can come back at any point and say that she didn't understand what she was signing, was under duress, and so forth. There is no way to legally "force" someone to stay in touch or be available to meet someone else in the future.

What to consider as an intended parent going into this is that the young women who become egg donors are indeed young, and any number of things may change over the years, including their willingness to meet the offspring of their egg donation cycles. Regardless of her intentions going into the donation, she may simply change her mind. That's something that all recipient parents must be willing to accept.

Does Your Agency Facilitate Anonymous, Open, or Both Kinds of Egg Donations?

Most egg donor agencies these days facilitate both kinds of donations. Typically, the intended parents express their interest in working with a donor who is accepting of being "known," and the donor is approached at that time to see if she is willing to pursue that type of relationship with the intended parents.

There is an FDA-required law stating that if a donor has lived in Europe at any time during 1980–1996, she must be a "known" donor. Intended parents must meet donors they've selected who meet this criteria and sign an affidavit stating that they understand the potential risks of mad cow disease being passed on to their offspring. If a donor lived in Europe during this time frame for five years or more, they are excluded from donating in the United States altogether.

What Type of Complications Insurance Does the Agency Provide for the Donor and What Are the Terms?

The most common egg donor insurance policies cover the donor up to $250,000 should there be any complications as a direct result of the egg donation procedure. You should be able to obtain a copy of the policy from your chosen agency for your records. These policies are typically taken out as soon as your donor starts her first injection and maintained for four months after that point.

All egg donation agencies have a responsibility to help their intended parents obtain their egg donors' complications insurance policy for the cycle. If an agency or IVF clinic does not provide a referral to companies providing complications insurance policies, this should be a point of concern because you do not want to end up being responsible for paying out of pocket in the event of unforeseen complications. The most common complication is *ovarian hyperstimulation*, which rarely, but occasionally, requires a donor to go to the emergency room for IV fluids and/or pain medication. If she ends up having an overnight stay, the cost could add up quite a bit. Other rare complications would include infection or ovarian torsion. Having a copy of your donor's insurance policy will help you understand what's covered and help protect you in the event of these rare yet potentially costly instances.

We'll review this in greater depth in Chapter 7 as well.

Who Coordinates the Legal Contract between the Intended Parents and the Egg Donor?

The rules governing egg donation procedures will vary from state to state. Although we can't speak to what international intended parents will experience when going through a donation procedure overseas, we can let you know what international recipients will experience as a general rule when coming to the States for egg donation cycles.

Most states require that an egg donor and their intended parent(s) sign a legal contract, although those who have no mention of an egg donation law at all will likely not require this. The legal contract is designed, as all contracts are, to protect both parties—in this case, both the egg donor and the intended parent(s). For that reason alone, it is strongly advised that you always enter into a signed agreement together regardless of your state's current legislation. Your contract with your egg donor should outline

- Egg donor pain/suffering/time compensation, travel and medication reimbursement, and cancellation fees
- The donor relinquishing her rights to the eggs and/or child(ren) as a result of the donation
- Obligation of both parties to maintain the others' privacy now and in the future
- Who the legal parents of the resulting child(ren) will be

Most agencies or IVF clinics have a list of attorneys with whom they have worked with before and come highly recommended. Some agencies will even have worked out agreed upon fees for clients they refer to certain attorneys as a result of the long-standing repeat business. Keep in mind that you do not have to use the attorneys recommended by your agency (because it is illegal to force someone to use any one attorney), although some will erroneously state that you must use only their attorneys. Our recommendation is to research the attorneys your agency or IVF clinic uses and choose the one with whom you feel most comfortable. The upside? You'll be working with an attorney familiar with the agency's policies and is therefore able to help move things along quickly and with ease.

In other cases, there are in-house attorneys who work directly for the agency. In these cases, you will have to sign a conflict of interest waiver. It's simple: An attorney should be working for you and your interests, but they happen to be on the payroll of the agency coordinating your cycle. This is where the waiver comes into play. The attorney's direct employment by the agency in no way suggests that they will act in any way that is not fair or ethically sound. It does, in legalese, create an obvious *potential* conflict of interest. If you're not presented with one of these waivers when working with an agency using an in-house attorney, it is perfectly within your rights to request one.

Occasionally, we have an intended parent who requests to work with an attorney (usually a family member or close friend) who is not familiar with egg donation law. We can't recommend strongly enough to avoid this situation. You've come so far on your journey that it's foolhardy to entrust your goals to an attorney inexperienced in the realm of the reproductive law in your state. Just because someone understands light bulbs doesn't make them an electrician. Skip the family friend and entrust your legal need in this case to someone educated and experienced in protecting you and your family's interests.

It is rare that an IVF clinic will start a cycle without legal contracts in place; however, it has been known to happen—especially in states where there are no current governing laws. It would then fall on you as the intended parent to require that a legal contract between you and your donor be drawn. Your responsibility would be to pay the legal fees between both you and your egg donor.

To close, we've asked one of our legal colleagues to weigh in with his views on contracts for your egg donation cycle. Steven W. Lazarus is an attorney in California whose practice is limited exclusively to the area of family formation law in which he handles hundreds of ART matters per year. In addition to practicing law in ART for close to 15 years, Steven is also an adjust law school professor in family formation law, has been a lead attorney responsible for the drafting and implementation of ART legislation in California, and is a frequent speaker at ART conferences, seminars, and in-services.

1) Reason Legal Contract is Needed for Egg Donor Cycles

There are numerous reasons why a legal contract is needed. Foremost, it is essential for a contract to specify that the recipients are the intended parents of the child(ren) conceived from the donated eggs and that the donor has no rights or responsibilities to the child(ren). The contract is also important to delineate, among other things, the intended parents' ownership of the resulting eggs and embryos, the respect liabilities of the parties (i.e., in the event of any medical complications to the donor), the consideration paid to the donor, and the confidentiality/anonymity of the arrangement.

2) Risks in Using a Clinic's Standard Contract or In-House Agency Contract

It must be abundantly clear that the contract is between a specific egg donor and specific intended parents who should be specifically identified in the contract by actual names or (if an anonymous arrangement), by first names, initials, pseudonyms, or code numbers. Frequently, the clinic standard contract and agency's in-house contracts are entered into between the party and the clinic/agency, rather than directly between the parties, and thus no actual privity of contract exists between the parties. It is also for the protection of all parties that each party consults with an attorney of his/her choice, and that the parties are aware of and have the opportunity to request any special provisions in the contract. Lastly, one of the recent landmark cases in California (which resulted in years of litigation among the parties) emanated in large part from the fact that a standard and unintended clinic document was used.

3) State Laws Regarding ART

All states do not have the same statutes, case law, and/or procedures with respect to assisted reproduction technology. The contract should specify which state's laws apply, and the particular state should have some nexus with the egg donation arrangement (i.e., the agency, one or more parties, and/or the clinic should be in the state whose laws are being used). Because the contract will fall under the laws of a particular state, at least one involved attorney should be licensed in that state and knowledgeable in its laws.

4) Common Requested Changes to the Contract

The most commonly requested change to the contract (whether placed in an addendum or in a revised contract) from an egg donor is with respect to the disposition of unused eggs and/or embryos. Frequently, the donor is not comfortable with excess eggs/embryos being donated to third parties for the purpose of conception or medical research. The most commonly requested change from the intended parents is adding some mechanism for future contact between the intended parents and the child (whether to facilitate any future exchange of medical information and/or a future meeting between the egg donor and the child).

5) Cases in Which Egg Donor Wants Custody of the Child(ren)

In the over 1,000 egg donation matters I've handled, not once has an egg donor wanted or even threatened to want custody of the child(ren). Any such dispute is more likely to occur when it's not clear from the outset who is intended to be the parent(s) of the child(ren). For instance, such disputes have occurred (although never in one of my cases) when the person providing the eggs is the partner of the carrier of the child(ren) and/or otherwise participates in the parenting of the child(ren). In California and many states, the intended parents are protected by the strong case law holding that whomever is intended to be a parent at the time of conception should be deemed an actual parent, regardless of the genetic makeup of the child(ren).

Does Your Agency's Fees Change Depending on Our Method of Payment (e.g., Cash, Credit Card, Wire Transfer, Check)?

It is our opinion that there should be no monetary difference in your fees, regardless of the method you use to pay your agency and donor. We would also be wary of agencies that offer reduced fees for payments made in cash.

"I think one of the most important things is for the agency you're working with to really talk with you about your donor. From what they are like to letting you know they'll stay on top of their taking their meds, and knowing that the donor is committed and responsible. Also to give you an overview about the things that will come next (and the costs)—the lawyer, the psychological exam, the genetic information, the drug costs later. Anything to make you feel informed and put your mind at ease would be ideal."—*Anonymous intended mother*

How Is the Recipient Parent Protected if the Egg Donor Does Not Take Her Medications as Agreed?

The biggest concern intended parents have is that a donor will forget an injection, take the wrong amount, or store them incorrectly. In the last 12 years that Wendie has been working in the field of assisted reproduction, she can count on one hand the number of times a donor has taken her medication incorrectly. It's rare for several reasons. First, because your fertility clinic's job is to teach your donor the correct way to take her injections (along with proper dosage) and follow up with her to be sure she understands. There's typically a written and/or verbal agreement with your donor at your fertility clinic indicating she understands everything required of her and her medication cycle. Second, the donor is aware prior to ever taking her injections that she would be in breech of contract if she takes her prescribed medications incorrectly.

Medication snafus can happen, and in the event that they do, you'll be contacted by your physician's office and/or your donor agency. Should you find yourself in the position that your donor's error will result in canceling the cycle, the donor should not receive any of her donor fee (as she is in breech of contract). This is another reason it's wise to ask your agency about their policy on donor fee advances. Some agencies will advance a donor a partial amount of her fee once she starts suppression hormones and then again on stimulation start. We personally find this practice to be too risky for intended parents in case of the rare instance a donor ends up in breech of contract. Ask any agency that has a policy of giving donor advances if, in the event of breech, the agency will then be responsible to pay you back for the donor's advance. If not, you should consider an addendum in your contract with your donor that if she is found in breech of contract after her advance, she will be legally responsible for immediately paying you back.

Now, because we've done a good job of scaring the bejesus out of you talking about donors in breech of contract, we want to reiterate that the *least* likely thing to happen during an egg donation cycle is breech of contract. Donors have no motivation, as they will not receive any money and could even potentially be obligated to pay lost funds back. Not to mention, most donors feel very connected to their intended parents and are nothing short of excited about helping them have a child. Nonetheless, it is important to ensure that your contract with your donor clearly spells out terms and remedies for breech of contract. It's important to all of you.

"I talked with two other agencies and didn't really vibe with the people I talked to. I knew I'd found the right agency when I got on the phone with the owner, and they understood what a momentous decision this was for me. I was never made to feel like a pain, even though I knew I was being one! I asked a lot of questions and took my time (and several deep breaths). When it was time to choose my donor, I knew it would be with this agency. Looking back, once I chose the donor, everything else was easy. Now I have healthy twins and not a single regret, only feelings of love and gratitude." —*Anonymous intended mother*

IN CLOSING: FEELING GOOD

An agency's job, above and beyond anything else, is to make this part of your journey as stress free and as enjoyable as possible. You should have a good gut feeling about the egg donor agency you choose and feel as though you are connected to the people who will be working with you over the coming months to help achieve your dreams. It is not uncommon to see some unexpected delay or small quirk to happen in each cycle due to the multiple variables involved, these are times where we can—as agency representatives and recipients alike—share in the humanity of what we're all working toward. Sometimes it's laughter, other times it's a smile. Just know that, whichever agency you choose, they want your smile and laughter to be more abundant than any other experience in your journey.

Key Chapter Highlights—How to Choose an Egg Donor Agency

- Be sure to ask plenty of questions as you interview prospective agencies.
- Make sure you understand how the agency will handle your donation cycle from both a logistical and financial standpoint.
- If you find it helpful, ask your agency for referrals from previous intended parents.
- Be sure you LIKE your egg donor agency.

6

Choosing Your Donor

Well, we've come to it, haven't we? The part where we talk about finding the perfect donor. It's a book about egg donation, right? To avoid mincing words, we'll share one important thing for you to remember up front: *There is no such thing as the perfect egg donor.*

Ideally, that perfect donor would be *you* and we understand that. So throughout this chapter, we'll help you through the journey of finding the next best thing to you—eggs from a wonderful young woman who represents so many qualities you admire and who will offer you the opportunity to build the family of your dreams.

The reasons you seek an egg donor aren't reasons that should make you feel isolated. Rather, they're not unlike the reasons other people need to seek egg donors. Together, you represent a segment of the world's population that yearns for family and will go to incredible lengths to see those dreams realized. We admire you for the strength and perseverance you've shown in your journey to this point and hope that the information that follows will offer you even more strength, warmth, and reassurance as you evaluate donors.

DON'T LET THE CHOICES OVERWHELM YOU

I remember about eight or nine years ago, shortly after I had started in this industry, I was working with an intended mother named Joanne. She was so stressed out and brokenhearted by the process of choosing a donor that it was practically destroying her ability to find daily happiness or even be able to function or talk without sounding like a frazzled mess. We spent quite a bit of time on the phone discussing donors, and I remember my heart feeling heavy, wondering if there was a way I could make her process any easier.

During that time in the egg donation industry, there was not the convenience of online donor databases, so we had to send entire copies of profiles along with photocopied photos on a sheet of paper. At one point, Joanne called me from downstairs to ask if I could come pick up all of the profiles she had viewed because none of them were right for her. When I arrived in the parking lot, she was trying to unload a whole stack of donor profiles from her car on what was a particularly windy day. When she turned around to give them to me, the profiles went flying around the parking lot, pictures and all! We spent the next 20 minutes chasing them down until we'd gathered the last one, at which point she just slumped on the ground and started sobbing. All she kept saying over and over is, "I just can't take any more, I just can't take any more. How could I possibly choose the right person to be my donor?"

Interestingly enough, the donor who was on the very top of the stack we'd rescued from the wind was someone I had just interviewed about a week before. What struck me as interesting was the polarity between Joanne in this moment and the donor. The donor was an adorable, happy, easy-going, peaceful young woman who seemed to embrace life's chaos with a grain of salt. I was thinking how badly I wished that a little bit of that calmness and internal peace would flow from this donor profile directly into Joanne and give her that sense of hope and calm that needed to come to allow the donor selection process to happen.

I told Joanne that she should go home, take an evening to just relax, and practice some deep breathing. I encouraged her to consider speaking with someone about this process and how to handle the inevitable stress that comes with it. I also took the donor profile I was holding and asked her, as a favor to me, to look at it again when she was in a calmer place.

About one week later, Joanne called me and told me that she was choosing this donor. Her voice sounded calmer, and she seemed to have that hope that comes with knowing you have made a good decision.

Jump to one year later, Joanne e-mails me photos of her healthy, gorgeous twin girls. About six months after that, I talked to her on the phone and listened to her gush about her twins' progress, personalities, and physical traits. She was happy, peaceful, and had an air of patience about her that was so calming I felt relaxed just being on the phone with her. It suddenly occurred to me that she reminded me *exactly* of her donor's personality when I first interviewed her. I kept thinking to myself, "If only I could show people their futures!"

Your story is your own, and every intended parent goes through a certain level of soul-searching as they approach the point of selecting an egg donor. Joanne's story represents how overwhelming it can be for intended parents to be faced with a selection of donors and having to ultimately choose *one*. What we can tell you is that there are a few things you can do and embrace to make the process of choosing a donor less stressful. And it all begins with taking a leap of faith.

THE LEAP

The very first thing to recognize is that there is only so much information you or your egg donor agency will be able obtain about your donor. However, there is also only so much that we can (and should) ask a donor. Partly because agencies don't want to be so invasive that our ability to attract donors to assist our intended parents becomes hindered but also based on practicality. We'll ask you to think of the friends you have in your life—the best of your best friends. How much do you know about them? What would you be comfortable asking? Although some friendships know no limits, there are certain things that people are definitely entitled to keep private—and as well, we all should! If you keep this in mind as you start to peruse donor profiles and those additional questions start wandering into your mind, you'll be able to build a conscientious list of questions whose answers are the most important to allow you to make the best decision.

WHAT KIND OF INFORMATION DOES AN EGG DONOR AGENCY REQUEST FROM DONORS?

Agencies do a fairly thorough job of acquiring the information that you and your fertility specialist will need to coordinate a successful cycle and feel confident in your selection. Although agencies do differ in the extent of information they gather, the following is a list of essential information that any agency or in-house donor roster should be able to provide about any young woman on their roster:

- Family and personal medical history (to the best of your donor's knowledge or ability to obtain)
- Recent pelvic exam records
- If listed, standardized test scores (SAT/ACT)
- College transcripts to verify enrollment or degrees earned
- A list of questions designed to tell you more about the donor's personality, likes, passions, and other important life events and talents

Something we frequently hear from intended parents is an inquiry about how factual a donor's self-provided medical history can be. In all honesty, it's as truthful as she is willing to make it, which is why no credible agency will fail to substantiate a donor's file with additional genetic counseling with a licensed geneticist. The additional genetic counseling involves a trained geneticist meeting with your donor to review her family medical history and indicate if they feel additional diagnostic testing should be performed prior to allowing the donor to donate. Additionally, many agencies will also have donors take a psychological evaluation (the MMPI, for example) to confirm she falls within the normal limits of a typical egg donor and therefore expect that the information she is providing is also likely truthful (please refer to Chapter 7 for additional information).

If you select a repeat donor, she will likely have had all or most of her genetic testing completed. First-time donors generally undergo their additional genetic screening following their selection by an intended parent. Why not prior to initial selection? Genetic testing can be costly, and there's no reason to submit donors to unnecessary blood tests or time commitments if they are not going to be selected to donate (because the majority of donors on rosters across the country will never be selected).

Your fertility clinic will test your donor prior to cycling for common things such as the presence of controlled substances like drugs or alcohol, communicable diseases, and some genetic carrier gene traits. The important thing to remember here is that everyone involved in helping you build your family is just as concerned about your donor's health and integrity as you are and will do everything possible to help you avoid these stresses in your decision-making process. Everything else above and beyond that will be a leap of faith.

WILLINGNESS TO MEET

As we've discussed previously in this book, there are two ways to go about an egg donation arrangement: anonymously or through a known donor. At the beginning of the egg donor industry, it was rare for intended parents to meet their donors. Over the past several years, however, there are coming to be more and more cases of intended parents who desire to meet their egg donors. With the growing support group network and increase in counseling professionals specializing in fertility-related cases, this isn't surprising, and for those of us in the industry, it's a beautiful development that can make the process even more meaningful for both donor and parent.

Why would you consider using a known donor instead of one who wishes to remain anonymous? Perhaps it's something about your personality that makes a young woman willing to meet more attractive as a donor. Maybe it's simply the ability to have an additional bond with her beyond her donor profile. Using a known donor gives you the option to openly communicate with your donor about your experiences and, should you be blessed, your child they helped create. For the donor, it can be a beautiful experience to meet with their intended parents and give them the unique opportunity to see firsthand the lives they are impacting with their gift. Although there is no way to guarantee that your donor will be willing to meet your child or with you in the future even though she is willing now, you can move forward knowing that you hold a more personal experience with your donor—regardless of what the future brings.

Erika's Story of Being a Known Donor

I've only been a known donor once during my multiple donations and it was at the request of the intended parents. Would I be willing to meet? Of course. Today, they've chosen to continue including me in family updates (complete with the latest pictures), and it's awe-inspiring for me to see this beautiful girl thrive. While this might not be a relationship that's right for every donor, I can't think of what my life would be like without it. Does it make the cycles I did being an anonymous donor any less special? Of course not. There's a certain smile I get when I think of the parents who get to look down at their children each night—children that I helped them create—and that itself is something I wouldn't trade for the world.

While the psychologists in assisted reproduction are strongly in favor of intended parents choosing to have an open relationship with their egg donors, we recognize that this doesn't work for everyone. Sometimes there are cultural or family constraints that don't make open donations easy. Some feel as though it will be too personal or emotional or that they'll think of their donor every time they see their child. Similarly, not every donor wants to meet her intended parents. If you want to work with a donor and feel very strongly about meeting, yet the donor doesn't feel comfortable proceeding, we wouldn't recommend that you force the issue. A meeting between donor and intended parent(s) is something that should be filled with joy and excitement, not dread from one party or another. There are plenty of donors who will agree to being known, and should your first choice in donor not be one of them, your agency should work diligently with you to find one that meets this important criterion.

"I wanted to make certain that I picked the best donor, so my children had an amazing life including health, intelligence, kindness, drive, spunk, with similar ethnic background and physical traits. I was fortunate that the agency I used provided a multitude of pictures, including adult photos of my donor. I also had an amazing lunch meeting with my egg donor, convincing me she was the perfect choice. I am creating a photo book including the donor's essays, background information, and other details so the girls will be well informed when they're ready." —*Recipient single mother of twin girls*

When is the right time to meet a prospective donor? When you've narrowed down your choices to your one favorite donor, that's the time to request a meeting through your agency. For most intended parents who want to meet with their chosen donor, that meeting is the last 1% of information they need to feel 100% certain with their choice. Your agency can make recommendations based on your respective locations if you're meeting outside of their offices and many agencies will facilitate your meeting on-site.

If you do decide that meeting your donor is right for you, here are some guidelines to help the process run more smoothly:

1. If you are meeting outside of your agency's offices, use a public place that will allow for privacy. A café, local park, or a private room at your doctor's office are all great places.

2. If you have a partner, both of you should meet your donor together. Raising children in a partnership takes a lot of support and togetherness, starting at the very beginning. Showing this support of one another to your donor will make the meeting and the experience better for everybody involved.

3. Be prepared with questions that are important to you. If you think you might get emotional or nervous and forget what you wanted to ask, write them down. Keep the questions light in nature and not like an interrogation. For example, asking a donor what she was like as a child is a great question. Asking your donor for her home address or where she goes to work everyday is not.

4. Be prepared for questions your donor may have for you. Decide ahead of time how much information you're comfortable disclosing, and keep your responses within your personal boundaries.

5. If you have all agreed to stay in touch in the future, wait until after the cycle is completed and there is a positive pregnancy before exchanging personal information. If you are meeting before the cycle starts, don't hand out your phone number or e-mail just yet.

6. Plan on the meeting lasting an hour or less. Keep in mind that you don't actually know your donor, so you don't want to be in a position of having uncomfortable silences or awkward moments. Think short, sweet, and to the point!

7. Consider having someone from your agency or doctor's office mediate. Most agency owners or their executives have had years of experience introducing donors and their intended parents. They can help stimulate the questions and keep the flow going throughout the meeting. They can also wrap the meeting up easily and work with you to share follow-up information as requested.

8. If you are meeting the donor in person, bring her flowers or a little token of your appreciation. This is an immediate icebreaker, showing that you took the time to think about doing something for her without even knowing her.

9. If you want to meet your donor but don't feel comfortable doing it in person or can't due to location, consider a telephone conference call or Skype. Your agency can moderate digital meetings, too.

Through the years, Wendie estimates that she's mediated close to 100 meetings between donors and their intended parents and to date, she's never seen one go badly. Both sides are usually pleasantly surprised to get to know one another and what results is a beautiful experience where people who—a moment ago—didn't know one another and are now coming together to create something incredible.

DON'T PUT ALL OF YOUR EGGS IN ONE BASKET

We hope you'll pardon the cliché, but it's perfect for the donor selection process. As much as we all wish it weren't the case, the process of selecting a donor is one filled with imperfections. There is no absolute guarantee that, even with using an egg donor, that you'll become pregnant on your first transfer. So that means that pinning all of your hopes on one particular donor can set you up for disappointment even before you've begun your cycle. It's a red flag for agencies when they meet with intended parents who say something like 'If this doesn't work I am done, I can't take it anymore!' Or they've looked at several thousand donors at various agencies, and the only person they found for them is *this one donor*. To an agency, that tells us that most likely, two things are going on:

1. They probably aren't ready to be parents if their requirements are so stringent that it took several thousand profiles before someone was "good enough" to be their donor.

2. We are already concerned that the intended parents haven't taken into consideration what they will do if this first cycle doesn't work. If they're of the mindset that there is only one donor who fits the bill out of thousands they've reviewed, how will they possibly cope if the donor doesn't pass her medical screening or produce enough eggs to make it to retrieval?

It's important to keep in mind that although agencies in the United States generally maintain generous rosters of donors on their Web sites, there is no guarantee on that donor's current availability or ability to complete the process. She might get a new job with no flexibility shortly before you decided you want to move ahead. She might have *just* been matched with a different couple. She might not pass her psychological, genetic, or medical screening. The best thing you can do for yourself is go to the donor selection process with a degree of emotional flexibility. When making a list of donors you feel would be great fits for the things you find to be most important, have at least two or three donors on that list. In the off chance that one of your selections is unavailable for whatever reason, having a few choices to look toward instead keeps you from going back to the emotional stress of reevaluating donors yet again. Also realize that agencies are placing new donors on their rosters all the time, and any great agency will be more than happy to let you know if they've found a new candidate that fits your bill.

Remember that regardless of whom you choose to be your donor, *your child will be perfect once they're in your arms.* We understand how overwhelming it can be to be presented with so many choices. Being given so much of a choice is sometimes a disservice to us. If a beautiful baby was put in your arms tomorrow, you would not, in that moment, care whether the egg that created him or her was not from your first choice of donor. Just look forward to the day where none of the difficult choices you are facing now will matter. You will just be a mom or a dad who is desperately in love with their child!

I am just blown away that such a young girl can put herself in my place and have so much true compassion for another. She's such a good girl, and I am really lucky to have her as my donor. When I was looking at her, besides being smart, interesting, ambitious, cute, organized, and focused (be still my organized, cross-off-the-list beating heart!), what really touched me and connected me with her were the pictures she sent of her with the red paint on her cheeks and the ones with her and her family. It told me volumes. The red paint on her cheeks told me that despite getting into a good college, majoring in a difficult major, getting the grades, and making her way in her field of choice during a very difficult historic global recession, that she was a goofy goof ball. Yes, very important. So you're pretty and smart, that's fine—the fact that you can be a goofy goof ball—well, very important in my book!

And the pictures of her family, talk about radiating love and just really enjoying each other's company; that is exactly how my family is. And that love that she was given is exactly what she is showing me right now. Every time I looked at a donor, I imagined her as a little girl and then a teenager and thought, would this be someone that I would want to live with (not to be funny here, but I really thought about that as I am very close to my niece and nephew and hung out with them when they were little and that bond is still strong as ever!). Was my kid going to be smart, interesting, passionate, funny, but most of all, kind? Were they going to be that pretty girl that was more concerned with getting the A than if that popular boy liked them? When my child turned 50 and the looks and body weren't what they used to be, were they going to have a brain to fall back on, a character that was going to make the world a better place, and a partner that they loved and loved them and their own kids that they dug? And our donor was an unequivocal yes to all of these thoughts. —*Recipient unmarried couple*

PERSONALITY, EDUCATION, HEALTH, AND PHYSICAL CHARACTERISTICS

Now that you know it's a good idea to have a few donors you like on your final list, how do you get to the processes of narrowing down your choices? What criteria do you use to begin making your selections? The most basic criteria where we see most intended parents focus their efforts are donor health, physical appearance, education, and personality. Of course, these vary in importance for all intended parents, but they're a great place for us to begin addressing the evaluation process of potential egg donors for you and your family.

Health

If a donor was the identical twin of the intended mother or had the beauty of a supermodel with an Oxford education, none of it would matter if she had a family health history that showed something potentially adverse. Simply put, poor health history trumps all other attributes for most intended parents in the donor selection process.

It's rare that you'll ever be presented with a donor who has a questionable health history, as most agencies do their best to screen out donors whose histories would be considered a red flag to fertility professionals and intended parents alike. For instance, a family history of Down syndrome, excessive cancer, young-onset strokes or heart issues, chronic depression/bipolar disorders/schizophrenia, seizures, autoimmune disorders, and so forth would almost always disqualify an egg donor. After all, you want to give your future child the best chance at life, and starting with a game of genetic roulette should be avoided at all costs. On the other hand, you also can't expect a donor (any donor) to have a perfect health history. Most people, if they really think about it, have a fair share of health issues hanging from their own family tree. The majority of intended parents Wendie has met with over the years will share that they have, perhaps, a grandmother who smoked or an uncle who struggled with alcoholism. What *you* need to decide is what you can live with and keep your expectations for your donor's health history reasonable. Looking for perfection is futile as, again, we are all human.

We asked Amy Vance, a board-certified geneticist, what basic guidelines she could offer for intended parents reviewing donor medical histories.

> The key thing I would advise to look for in your egg donor's medical history would be a family history free from genetic disease, birth defects, mental retardation, autism, mental health issues, learning disabilities, or other multifactorial conditions, especially in close relatives. The closer the relative, the higher the risk. I would stay away from family histories of disease where the disease is repeated many times in the family. Most of all, I would advise to try to find a donor with a family history that you're comfortable with, since all families have some diseases. I would make sure that I was well informed about the family history and associated risk, so that I was making as informed a decision as possible and I had no regrets going forward.

Be sure to consult Appendix D regarding genetic testing for donors for more information on donor health histories.

Physical Characteristics

Almost every intended parent initially starts their search asking for donor candidates who have similar features, ethnicity, and coloring to their own. One of the most important parts of being able to connect with an egg donor as you narrow down your selections is finding ones who you feel offer an excellent physical representation of the genetic materials you're replacing: you. The last thing most people want to worry about is whether people will think your child looks like you or not. Although it's none of their business whether your child looks like you or not, it still causes most intended parents to, at least initially, seek out someone who shares some of their more prominent features. I've had donors chosen because they looked like an intended parent's relative or were very similar in features to one parent or the other.

To allay any curiosities or fears, it is not common practice for agencies to help intended parents "engineer" their children by allowing them to select donors who are vastly different from them on a physical level. Ethnic considerations are taken into account as well as prominent characteristics, like matching a 6′1″ blonde donor with brunette parents who are both short in stature. When you begin reviewing donor physical characteristics, it can help to make a list of the lovely features that you possess and would like to find in your children. A quirky nose, beautiful almond-shaped eyes, prominent chin, or dimples are all things to put on the list, and even without the list, you'll be able to spot these things at 100 paces as you begin review-ing potential donors.

"Not only was our donor incredibly lovely, but we were particularly impressed with her family background because she has things in common with ours both in terms of education and exposure. These things together made it an easy choice." —*High-profile married couple*

Education

This has come to be such an important consideration for most intended parents that most egg donation agencies feature an entire search category on their Web sites to those who have achieved higher than average academic success.

If a donor goes to or has graduated from an Ivy League college or another institution that is nationally recognized as one of the better schools in the country (both in the United States and abroad), they will likely be asked by the agency or intended parents to provide their transcripts. Additionally, the more educated the donor, the more likely it is that she will have easy access to her SAT or ACT scores because those would be important for her acceptance to these schools. Most agencies request standardized test scores on their initial donor applications but do not require proof unless the scores are of an exceptional level. Of course, you're welcome to ask your agency to see if they can acquire further corroboration for educational achievement claims from a donor, but understand that requests like these can delay the selection process, your cycles, and cause you unnecessary stress if you're relying on this information alone to select the best donor.

Is there a genetic guarantee that the children of high-achieving donors will follow in their footsteps? Of course not. However, those intended parents who themselves achieved academic success tend to prefer donors who have achieved the same.

Personality

You might find it curious, but we tend to see intended parents placing more and more weight on a donor's personality. For this reason alone, we always suggest that you don't go into your donor search with such specific require-ments that the search engine only finds one or two donors who fit all your criteria. For example, if you type in as your search category: brown hair, green eyes, 5′6″, high academic achiever, athlete, previous donor, likes Douglas Adams, prefers the ocean to the mountains, and is located in Oregon—chances are you will get *maybe* one donor, more likely none. If you add some flexibility to your search and choose

- green, blue, or hazel eyes
- blonde, brown, or auburn hair
- height range 5′4″–5′8″

you're more likely to receive several donors returned in your search results to begin evaluating. But what about personality?

This is when the next important factor comes in to play, but it comes down to which donors do you *like*. Who do you feel you would be friends with? Who would make you laugh or has the same taste in books or movies? Do you see a donor in particular who seems to share core values and motivations in her life as you have in yours?

A child's personality is no more a given than a child's academic prowess. However, these are the choices that will make you more comfortable with the donor you choose to help you on this journey. Although you might not have considered it before, it certainly helps to like the person who is going down this path with you. And although it may not be the initial important factor for choosing a donor at the *beginning* of your search, you might be surprised at how much liking a person, even if she isn't an exact physical match, makes a huge difference in your final choices.

DONOR STATUS: PREVIOUS AND/OR PROVEN DONOR VERSUS A FIRST-TIME DONOR

You may find yourself in a position where your fertility specialist makes the recommendation that you seek a previous or proven donor. This is oftentimes a factor of the journey you've taken thus far and the challenges your particular case faces. Other times, it simply is a preference of the fertility clinic or for intended parents who find comfort in knowing a donor they have selected has gone through the donation process before and, in some cases, helped create a pregnancy. Let's review the difference between previous and proven donors.

A *previous donor* is one who has successfully completed at least one donation cycle with acceptable results. By acceptable results, we'd call it that she had a good cycle or one where she stimulated well, produced more than 12 follicles, and had a good fertilization rate and resulting good quality embryos but one where no pregnancy resulted. Because there are so many factors that go into a positive pregnancy, the negative pregnancy outcome might have nothing to do with the quality of the donor's eggs and still places these donors in a separate category from first-time donors as "known quantities" for intended parents looking for more reassurance. As a multiple-time donor, Erika's very first cycle was highly successful, yet the intended parents did not achieve pregnancy. Had a fertility specialist not reviewed her cycle records when another intended parent who wanted to use her came along, it's pretty safe to say that several families wouldn't be looking at their incredible children today (and many of them multiples).

A *proven donor* is one who had not only completed a previous donation cycle but whose cycle created a pregnancy. Her cycle would be considered successful whether or not she had 7 eggs or 30 eggs retrieved so long as a viable pregnancy occurred. It's also very possible that your doctor may choose a donor who had a high-egg/embryo yield, but a negative pregnancy result over a donor with a low-yield and successful pregnancy if her cycle records indicate that her overall cycle was better in the instance of the high-yield/no pregnancy.

> The most important thing I can tell an intended parent is to find somebody that they feel comfortable with, which can be more intuitive than either looks or intelligence. I am okay with first-time donors, too. All good donors were a first-time donor in the past. There are things we can do to evaluate first-time donors to see how she'd do in a stimulation cycle. However, I will always choose a previous donor over a first-time donor if I'm given two donors to choose from and one has a history of good stimulation. I would look at this more than age. If I'm choosing between two first-time donors, I would choose based on age—that is, I would choose the 21-year-old donor over the 30-year-old donor.—*Bradford Kolb, MD, Huntington Reproductive Center*

But what about the first-time egg donor? With so many wonderful young women willing to share their genetic gift, it helps to remember that every proven or previous donor was once a first-time donor. First-time donors come from every walk of life imaginable and may or may not already have children of their own. The question is, "How do you know if she'll be a good donor?" With so many factors that go into a successful cycle, we'll help you work through the ones that can help you feel at ease with your choice of a first-time donor.

Your egg donor agency can help you review your donor's application and offer you their thoughts from their personal impressions as to why they feel a particular first-time donor might be a great fit for you. Her maturity level (regardless of age) can be easily gauged from her responses on her donor application, and the results of her MMPI or related psychological testing can help assure you that she has the level of responsibility required to be a compliant donor. Aside from the cooperation it requires on the part of a donor for a successful cycle, there are simply some things you won't know until you begin the stimulation process.

If you're curious about other tests your donor might be subject to in order for your fertility clinic to ensure she's progressing as needed, here is a breakdown of the most common tests and the optimal levels:

Follicle-stimulating hormone (FSH) levels: This is a fertility test of ovarian reserve. It is taken on Day 3 of your donor's menstrual cycle. When a woman stops producing enough estrogen in her ovaries, her FSH levels rise. A level higher than 10 mlu/mL generally means that the egg quality is starting to diminish. Most donors have FSH levels between 4 mlu/mL and 8 mlu/mL.

Estradiol or estrogen (E2) levels: This is taken on Day 3 of your donor's menstrual cycle. The opposite of FSH, when your ovaries stop producing estrogen, estradiol levels start to drop. Normal levels for donors will generally be 75 or less.

Antral follicle count/resting follicles/phasal follicle count (AFC): These are the number of small follicles that are visible via ultrasound in the ovaries. It is considered by many physicians to be a reliable predictor on how a donor will respond during the IVF cycle. Most donors will have an AFC of 16 or higher, although 10–15 is acceptable. More than 30 might indicate someone with polycystic ovarian syndrome (PCOS).

A growing number of physicians are also starting to use a few additional tests as a standard of practice with both first-time and previous/proven donors. These include the following:

Anti-Müllerian hormone (AMH): The AMH is secreted by the cells inside the follicles. It is considered a good indicator of the number of eggs that will likely be retrieved. A donor with high AMH levels usually result in a favorable egg yield, whereas low AMH levels often indicate poor response to stimulating medications.

Inhibin B test: This is the hormone secreted by the ovaries that controls the FSH. Inhibin B levels are reflective of ovarian reserve. You ideally want to see high inhibin B levels in egg donors because they are young with what should be substantial ovarian reserves. It's not industry standard to order this test, but its use is on the rise in the fertility industry.

Chlomid challenge test (CCCT): As Bradford Kolb, MD, of Huntington Reproductive Center explains, this is like a "stress test" on the ovaries. If FSH levels remain low, that's a good sign. If they increase dramatically, it can be a poor prognostic indicator for the quality for an egg donor cycle.

All of the earlier mentioned tests are not ordered as a standard of practice. Rather, there are the three most common (FSH/E2 and AFC), followed by the less common but sometimes seen AMH, chlomid challenge and inhibin B. It is best to ask your fertility clinic which tests it suggests, requires, and feels it would be beneficial to add any of the others suggested here for your donor of choice.

In summary, here are some pros and cons for both previous/proven and first-time donors for you to consider as you evaluate your options:

Pros for Previous/Proven Donors

- We know how previous donors respond to the stimulation medication.

- She passed all of her initial screening tests (i.e., testable genetic carrier genes, drug/alcohol/nicotine, STDs, or other communicable diseases).

- If she cycled recently, some of her screening tests may still be valid and thus save your money.

- She has proven herself reliable and committed, which is very reassuring for intended parents. The chance of her backing out is negligible, having been through the process before and realizing what is at stake.

- She knows how to take her injections.

- There is often a proven pregnancy or history of good stimulation and egg/embryo count.

- Previous medical records will be available to show your IVF clinic.

- Your doctor can vouch for her (unbiased) based solely on her medical history.

Cons for Previous/Proven Donors

- These donors will likely command a higher fee.

- She may not respond exactly the same every time to stimulation.

- She might have cycled more times than you are comfortable with (the ASRM recommends a cutoff of six cycles; however, some agencies and clinics will work with donors indefinitely as long as she is still achieving positive results).

- Some intended parents worry about their future offspring having multiple, yet unknown, half-siblings.

Pros for First-Time Donors

- Her donation gift is currently exclusive to only you, and she may decide to donate only once.
- She will likely ask a lot of questions and always double check that she's taking her medication correctly.
- She will likely take a lower fee.
- With a good health history, appropriate age, and a pretested FSH/E2 and AFC, she is likely to respond just as well as a repeat donor.

Cons for First-Time Donors

- It is unknown how she will respond to the stimulation medications.
- She will be learning how to take her injections for the first time.
- If she has never been pregnant or had kids of her own, there is no previous history of fertility.
- Medical screening fees will be higher as she will not have had any of the required donor testing completed and on file.

If you're having a difficult time choosing between a previous/proven and first-time donor, the preceding pros and cons will help you understand what's involved in using either type as you narrow down your donor choices. Regardless of which type of donor you choose to help you along this journey, just be sure before you start your cycle that you and your fertility clinic have the information you need to produce the most successful cycle possible.

DONOR FEES

We've discussed donor fees at various points of this book already, but here, we'll let you know what those fees include and things that should go into evaluating whether you feel a donor's profile justifies the fee she commands.

Most egg donor fees range from $5,000 to $10,000. It's rare to see fees less than $5,000 outside of in-house donor programs at fertility clinics and only a handful of donors will command more than $10,000. As stated in previous chapters, donor fees vary widely based on several factors:

- Previous cycle results
- Donor demand

- First-time donor status
- Agency rules/restrictions
- Out-of-town versus local donors

We'll review each of these criteria and their impact on the donor fee.

Previous Cycle Results

As an intended parent starting this process, it is reasonable to expect that a donor who has cycled multiple times with continued positive results will most likely command a higher fee. If a donor has had a previous cycle that resulted in a positive outcome (pregnancy), most agencies will then raise her fee or the donor will request/require it. Other agencies base the fee on the overall outcome and recovery time for each individual donor. For example, a donor who has consistent and exceptionally high egg yield and a higher chance of hyperstimulation or longer recovery period will likely request a higher fee, taking into account additional lost wages and recovery time.

Donor Demand

There are certain traits that are unusual or unique in the egg donor landscape and may lend a donor to be paid a higher fee. Perhaps she goes to an Ivy League college and the cost of tuition or living expenses are high enough to warrant a fee, which can help cover the expense. Or perhaps she has a high-paying job or one that requires her to take more than the normal time off if she commits to being an egg donor, causing her to request more money to justify her lost wages. Keep in mind that the more unusual or difficult it is to find a particular type of donor, the more likely it is that her demand will be such that you could be facing higher fees.

First-Time Donor

Most first-time donors are willing to accept a lower fee not only because they will be matched with intended parents quicker and be able to help someone have a family, but also because they don't know yet if this will be an easy or difficult process for them. The degree of discomfort and recovery time varies greatly from donor to donor. Although you may occasionally find a donor who strongly feels a higher first-time fee for her efforts is the only way she'd be comfortable moving forward, know that if you are on a budget that the majority of donors will be open and willing to taking a lower fee.

Agency Rules/Restrictions

Some agencies and in-house donor programs IVF clinics have caps on fees for first-time donors. For example, they may require that ALL first-time donors be willing to accept a fee of $5,000. Many agencies also have a cap on the highest amount they will pay a donor, period. Because of the ASRM suggested guidelines, you will more often than not see the donor fees max out in the $10,000 range. There are also many agencies that make exceptions for unique situations, whereas others who do not feel it's necessary to dictate what an egg donor can command for her time and efforts. It is not our intention to judge how each individual agency runs, rather our goal is to prepare you for the differences among agencies so that you aren't surprised by the fee variations.

Out of Town versus Local Donors

If you choose a donor in another state or far enough away that she cannot make appointments at your local clinic, fees for the cycle will increase. Here are the additional costs that might apply to an out-of-area donor, and we expand on this in Chapter 7 when we review the logistics of your cycle:

- **Monitoring facility:** Your donor will need to be monitored at a local IVF clinic for the majority of her midcycle appointments. Most (if not all) monitoring clinics charge a one-time coordination fee for this service. We've seen coordination fees range from $50 to $750 and everything in between. You will also be charged for any tests ordered directly from your own physician. Additionally, your own clinic may charge a flat rate for donor monitoring regardless of whether you are using their facility or an outside facility. Be sure to inquire about this if you're leaning toward an out-of-area donor.

- **Airfare:** Out of town donors will be required to make two trips to your clinic. The first one will be either a day or overnight trip for her initial consultation, screening, and evaluation. Her second trip will be for 5–10 days (on average) at the end of her cycle through retrieval (including 1–2 days recovery time). Many agencies require that donors bring a companion with them for safety reasons, so figure in the cost of additional airfare.

- **Hotel:** Your donor will need to stay at a hotel near your clinic. Most agencies use quality but reasonably priced hotels (think Sheraton, Holiday Inn,

Embassy Suites). Find out ahead of time if your donor will require a room with a refrigerator, Internet access, or other amenities and whether you will be responsible for payment. Most agencies require payment for room, tax, and parking only. Any additional amenities would be the responsibility of your donor and her companion.

- **Car rental:** Your donor will most likely need a car rental to make her appointments and drive herself to and from the airport during her stay for the initial consultation and retrieval period. Again, most agencies use quality, reasonably priced cars (usually 2–4 door, economy like a Corolla). If a donor wants to upgrade, she would be required to use her own credit card or obtain approval from the agency in advance. Typically, the car rental, insurance, and GPS would be covered. Also, some cities might be more conducive to using taxis instead of renting a car. In these instances, an estimated amount will be sent to the donor to cover the costs for cab fare to and from the airport and her doctor's visits.

- **Per diem:** All donors are given a travel stipend or per diem to be used (typically) for food, gas, and incidentals. This is usually broken down by the number of days traveled and sent to her about a week before her scheduled trip. We've seen the range for travel stipend as low as $50 per day and as high as $150, based on her destination city (with destinations like San Francisco or New York being on the higher end of the spectrum). If your agency requires a companion to travel with your donor, the per diem will likely be higher to cover the companion's food cost as well.

- **Lost wages:** A reasonable expectation for donors and intended parents alike is that she will be traveling approximately 5–7 days at the end of her cycle. Occasionally, a doctor's office will require closer to 7–10 days. In addition, if your donor is at high risk for hyperstimulation or had any other complications during her cycle that require an unexpected extended stay, an agency may require additional lost wages be paid to the donor above and beyond her cycle fee and per diem. Most likely this would be for travel over the expected time frame. The donor may be required to show a pay stub for proof of wages or the agency may just make it a flat rate regardless of whether the donor makes more or less.

On average, selecting an out-of-town donor will end up costing somewhere between $3,000 and $5,000 more than one in your local area, depending on where they are coming from and how long they're required to stay. Be prepared to either transfer the higher end estimate into an escrow account used by the agency or provide the agency (or their preferred travel service) with a credit card that will be used as needed for travel expenses throughout the cycle. You should be able to retain a full accounting at the end of the cycle as to the amounts paid and to whom or what service and if you are due a refund of any unused funds in the travel escrow account.

HELPFUL HINTS FOR YOUR DONOR
SELECTION PROCESS

We understand that all of these things that go into choosing a donor are enough to make your head swim. The important thing to remember is that once you're at the stage of reviewing donor profiles, let your instincts take control and you can explore the scientific practicalities once you're deeper into narrowing down your selections. Here are a few helpful hints that will make the beginning of your donor search easier:

- Go in with an open mind. Be flexible with certain physical attributes. If you have light eyes, be open to blue, green, or hazel. If you have brown hair, perhaps expand that to dark brown, black, or dark blond. The more specific you get, the fewer options you'll have from which to choose.

- If you have a partner or spouse or if you're single but are sharing the experience of your journey with a close friend or family member, ask them to go on the donor database separately and choose their top 10 favorite donors for you. You'll do the same. See if any of your top 10 choices include the same donor(s). Many donors have been chosen because both partners chose them independently of one another.

- Ask your agency to make suggestions. This is particularly helpful if you've had a chance to talk to them so they can get an idea of your personality. For example, if you are extremely athletic, they may have just interviewed a donor who loves the same sports or activities. Sending the agency a photo can be extremely helpful as they likely will have some suggestions if you are seeking someone who resembles you.

- Know the absolute maximum amount you are able to budget for the donor fee prior to starting the selection process. It can be disappointing to find the donor you want only to find out that you've budgeted for $7,000, and her asking fee is $10,000.

- Decide from the beginning if you are going to only look at previous/proven donors or if you're open to first-time donors as well.

- If you've looked at several hundred (or several thousand) profiles and still don't feel like anybody is "right" for you, consider the following:

  1. Are you sure you are emotionally prepared to move forward at this time, or are you putting obstacles in your path? If you suspect the latter, consider speaking with a therapist who specializes in third-party reproduction issues.

  2. Ask your agency if they will do a specialized search for you. Some will do this for free, and others will charge a small fee plus advertising costs.

3. Using a personal donor-matching service that specializes in finding hard-to-match clients their donors, usually by working with several agencies at a time.

4. Try using a national donor database, such as Donor Network Alliance (www.donornetworkalliance.com), to maximize your search.

- And lastly—like your donor. It always adds comfort to the process when you choose someone you feel you would be friends with or reminds you of someone you like. This should be an emotionally rewarding experience for you that puts you one step closer to the family of your dreams, not a stress-inducing process that keeps you up nights. Like your donor, because if you ever met, it's a solid bet she would probably like you, too.

CHECKLIST FOR INTENDED PARENTS PRIOR TO CONFIRMING A DONOR SELECTION

- Has she had a previous donation, and if so, was your doctor's office given all of the medical information needed to make an informed decision on your behalf?

- If you want to meet your donor, did she agree to this? Will you meet before, during, or after the cycle? Was there an agreement to future contact? What was agreed upon (i.e., will the contact go through the agency, clinic, attorney, e-mail, phone number exchange, or third-party donor/ sibling registry)?

- Is your donor okay with *you* making the choice on what to do with the remaining embryos (i.e., save them for future siblings, adopt them to another family, donate them to science, etc.)?

- Does your donor have any blackout dates (i.e., unchangeable vacations, school, work, or family obligations, etc.) that you need to be aware of that could impact your cycle schedule?

- Did your donor reconfirm that all of the information in her medical history was up-to-date and accurate?

- If she has unusually high SAT/ACT scores or goes to a prestigious college, was your agency able to obtain a copy of her scores or transcripts?

- Do you require a background check, and if so, were the results provided to you?

- Has your donor revealed to her family that she is donating? If not, will she proceed despite any objection should they find out during the course of the cycle?

- If she was a previous donor with your current agency, did they provide you with her genetic and psychological evaluations prior to the signing of your donor agreement and any money exchanging hands?

- If you have chosen a first-time donor and you are not comfortable with the results of her psychological and genetic evaluations, how much of your program fee is refundable? Is the donor given any portion of her fee for her time and efforts?

- If an unmarried donor has a sexual partner, is her partner willing to be tested for communicable diseases? If not, are you comfortable moving forward with only your donor being tested? Is her partner supportive? Are they okay with abstaining from sexual activity throughout the injection phase of the process?

- When was her last menstrual period start date?

- Did you both agree and finalize her fee? Is everything you need in writing with the agency?

We've also included this information in Appendix C for your reference along with additional donor-related questions.

Remember that, above and beyond anything else, this is your time to experience new hope and excitement about your future family. Choosing a donor can be stressful, daunting, and sometimes even disappointing; but it can also be exciting, (gasp!) enjoyable, and even give you the optimism and endurance it takes to carry on your dream of having a family. We hope you will ultimately enjoy the process and celebrate the gift that the young women from whom you have to choose are offering in the name of your dreams.

7

Circling the Nest—The Ovum Donation Cycle

O ne of the most common questions from intended parents is, "What happens once I choose a donor?" As most people coming into an egg donation scenario are unfamiliar with what comes next, we've built this chapter to offer you realistic expectations of the next steps, both medical and logical in nature. If you've opted to secure your donor through an egg donor agency, it's not uncommon to find that they will take your hand and walk you through this process step-by-step. While your fertility clinic and egg donor agency might handle things in a bit different order, what follows is a very normal order of events that you can use as a guide through your cycle. As always, your fertility clinic and donor/surrogacy agency should be there right by your side to answer questions and help you through this stage of your egg donor cycle with as little stress as possible.

PSYCHOLOGICAL EVALUATIONS AND GENETIC COUNSELING

Once you've selected your donor and she's been confirmed as able and willing to cycle, the next step will be to ensure she has the proper genetic and psychological screenings performed. If she is a previous donor, this may already have been done. However, if it has been over a year since the screenings have been performed, most agencies will contract a psychologist and geneticist to do follow-up evaluations to make sure nothing has changed since the donor's last cycle.

Psychological Evaluation

The standard for psychological evaluations in the egg donor world is the Minnesota Multiphasic Personality Inventory (MMPI), which is one of the most common tests given to assess and/or diagnose mental illness. There are certain parameters a donor must fall within to be cleared to move forward with an egg donor cycle (your agency and their psychological professional interpreting the test can provide their specific guidelines). Once your donor receives a satisfactory score on her MMPI, it is suggested by most ART psychologists and clinics to have an in-person follow-up with a licensed mental health professional based on her results. The reason for this is that although the MMPI may test for mental health issues, the person-to-person follow-up evaluation will also cover the issues that may arise specifically as a result of the egg donation process. Because many of the young women donating are in their early 20s, it's possible that they may not have considered the potential short- or long-term issues that might arise resulting from their donation. For example:

- Do they have empathy and an understanding of how much time, money, and emotions the intended parents are putting into using them as an egg donor?

- Will they be able to work their school/work/family obligations around the doctor's visits? Are they fully committed to making every appointment on time?

- If the cycle gets canceled prior to retrieval, do they understand that they will only be paid a partial amount of their retrieval fee and if they are in breech of contract for any reason, they will be paid no fee?

- Do they understand that they will be on hormones that may cause mood swings, bloating, and/or discomfort? Are they aware and okay with the potential complications such as hyperstimulation, infection, or reactions to the anesthesia?

- Do they understand that they will be taking daily injections and are they willing to self-administer their injections? What is their alternate plan if they find they cannot give themselves the shots?

- Do they have friends or family who will provide social support to them throughout the process and/or during their recovery period? Have they told anybody they are close to about being an egg donor?

- If the donor is married or in a committed relationship, do they have the support of their spouse/significant other?

- How will they feel about doing the donation later in life? Five years from now? What about ten years from now if they find out that, for some reason, they are unable to have or haven't yet had children of their own?

- Are they willing to meet the child and/or the intended parents? Do they want to receive updates on the pregnancy, birth, or the child? Are they okay if they don't get updates? Have they discussed these preferences with the agency prior to beginning the cycle?

Carole Lieber Wilkins, MFT, offers her thoughts about the importance of having an in-person evaluation after you receive the results of a donor's written MMPI.

> The psychological evaluation of donors has an educational component that is just as important as the psychological piece. A big part of the consultation process is helping women understand the lifelong consequences of their decision to donate. It should be emphasized that a *real* child may result from their participation. This ensures the potential donor can provide full informed consent, understanding the lifelong impact of her participation. The importance of this interview cannot be understated. Physicians do not prescribe medication without first examining a patient to determine the appropriateness of the prescription. In the same way, mental health professionals cannot evaluate the suitability of a donor for this huge commitment without meeting her. Through this evaluation, intended parents can feel confident that a trained professional has laid eyes on and had a conversation with the donor to ensure that she is honest and forthcoming, healthy, and fully understands her commitment. And donors gain the knowledge to truly make a decision about the lifelong nature of this commitment and understand what will be expected of them going forward. Only through having well-informed donors can we trust that a donor will stick with the process from start to finish and come out of it feeling positive and confident about helping someone have a long sought-after child.

If your clinic or agency does not require an in-person psychological evaluation follow-up to the MMPI, consider requesting one. Some psychologists also use Skype or phone calls as a follow-up to an MMPI, however it is generally considered ideal for the donor to meet the psychologist in person. It is not only to ensure that your donor is mentally prepared for the more immediate experience of your cycle, but it is also the best thing for her to go in fully informed and prepared for the possible long-term effects associated with egg donation.

Genetic Counseling

More clinics are now requiring that egg donors have a one-on-one evaluation with a licensed geneticist. A genetic evaluation is what the intended parents should know or ask about their donor (see Appendix D for a thorough checklist of questions typically asked by geneticists and additional information on testing).

Amy Vance, MS, CGC, a licensed Genetic Counselor and the founder of Bay Area Genetics, explains the importance of genetic counseling on all donors prior to their medical screening appointments, and why all agencies (and fertility clinics) should require this as soon as a donor is matched with her intended parent(s).

Genetic counseling is the process of helping people understand and adapt to the medical, psychological, and familial implications of genetic contributions to disease. This process integrates

- interpretation of family and medical histories to assess the chance of disease occurrence or recurrence
- education about inheritance, testing, management, prevention, resources, and research
- counseling to promote informed choices and adaptation to the risk or condition.

Having a thorough review and interpretation of the family medical history helps ensure that intended parents have not only complete information but also interpretation of potential risks to their offspring.

The purpose of genetic carrier screening is to identify couples at-risk for having an affected child so that they can make informed reproductive decisions. Carrier screening is traditionally offered based on the ethnic background or family history. Current guidelines for genetic testing set forth by the American Society for Reproductive Medicine (ASRM) and American College of Obstetrics and Gynecology include screening based on both ethnicity-based and family history but does not include multiplex genetic carrier screening.

A copy of the donor's family tree or "pedigree" is provided to the intended parents for their records. For a couple using an anonymous egg donor, this may be the most detailed information they receive about the medical history of their offspring's family.

On occasion, there is new information that comes up during the genetics consult that was not elicited by the donor's profile, or there is a positive genetic test result on the donor. These are difficult circumstances that may lead to the intended parent deciding not to go forward with the donor. Knowing this information prior to extensive medical testing and certainly prior to a pregnancy allows for the opportunity to make important decisions about moving forward.

Unfortunately, you cannot completely count on the donor's memory during the initial stages of filling out her application with your agency, the confidence that nothing medically has changed with her or her family since she filled out the application, or the thoroughness of your egg donation agency's medical checklist to reveal important genetic implications. Because agencies are typically not staffed with medical or genetic professionals, their ethical responsibility to rely on outside experts to perform additional genetic counseling is of the utmost importance (regardless of whether your doctor's office recommends this additional testing or not). The following are several examples where we have seen genetic counseling alert intended parents to potential abnormalities prior to a cycle moving forward:

Example 1: A donor's medical history showed very little in the way of medical concern. Upon being chosen to cycle, she was asked by the agency if anything had changed medically in her family since she signed up to be an egg donor. She stated nothing had. During her genetic counseling session, it was discovered that not only her mother but her own daughter had been diagnosed with epilepsy. When confronting the donor about this extremely important issue that directly affected her genetic history (and also would have kept her from being accepted in any egg donor program), she stated that she was positive this information had been revealed on her egg donor profile. Whether she just thought she included that information, but hadn't, or whether there was a computer glitch that caused the information to be deleted will never be known; however, the genetic counselor discovering this information prior to the cycle starting was extremely important.

Example 2: An intended father tested positive for one cystic fibrosis (CF) mutation, but after reviewing his personal history with a geneticist, he actually appeared to be affected. Even though he had not yet had the gene sequencing test to confirm he had it, he reported recurrent pneumonia, bronchitis, sinusitis, and salty sweat associated with CF. Therefore, it was essentially confirmed through genetic counseling that he had CF. The egg donor, who was Hispanic, was referred for the gene sequencing test for CF, only to find out she was a carrier. Had the donation proceeded, the intended parents would have been subject to a 50% risk for having an affected child. If they had not seen a genetic counselor, the intended father would most likely have not been diagnosed with CF prior to the donation cycle, and the donor might have only had a routine screening panel due to her low ethnic risk.

Example 3: There was an intended father with a strong family history of breast and ovarian cancer. Because it was on the father's side, nobody considered that this would be a potential risk to their offspring in the same way that it would have been had it been the intended mother with the family history. It is a common myth that the intended father's history is not important, but that is incorrect for the forms of breast cancer proven to be hereditary. Due to their interview with a geneticist, they were able to properly select a donor to help diminish this risk in their children.

Occasionally, intended parents will be extremely upset or feel as though they weren't given complete information by the agency when something comes up on the genetic counseling report of which they were previously unaware. Although sometimes it could be argued that it was the agency's negligence in obtaining complete information, the most important thing to remember is that the reason they use a genetic counselor to begin with is to catch what they may have missed or the donor unintentionally omitted from her medical background. Agencies do not (and cannot) have every donor meet with a genetic counselor at the time of being accepted into the program—it's simply a matter of cost. At any given time, an agency will have more than 200 donors on their roster who will never be chosen by intended parents. Thus, requiring a donor go through extensive (and costly) genetic counseling does not happen until she has been chosen to move forward with the egg donation process. It is my experience that, for agencies that require genetic counseling on their egg donors, the additional cost is typically included in the program fee or expenses.

COMPLICATION INSURANCE POLICY

Both you and your donor are now moving forward with the cycle with the hopes of the best possible outcome, but complications can sometimes arise for the egg donor who is dedicated to helping you achieve your dreams. When you receive your cycle schedule from your fertility clinic, you or your agency will need to take out the egg donor's Complication Insurance Policy (CIP). The average egg donor policy covers a donor for up to $250,000 in the case of an emergency directly related to the egg donation process. The insurance policy should also cover the donor in case of accidental death, including (but not limited) to such things as a car accident on the way to one of her required cycle appointments.

Because egg donation is an elective procedure, her current medical policy would not cover any complications as a result of egg donation. Most CIP's are considered "prime" policies, so that in the event of a complication, she will not have to submit the claim to her primary insurance first. In the event of an emergency, the donor would contact the insurance broker for the CIP and work with them directly to receive coverage and care for any complications and procedures required.

What is covered on your CIP? Here are some common scenarios:

- Ovarian hyperstimulation requiring hospitalization
- Allergic reaction to the medications taken for the cycle requiring hospitalization

- Infection as a result of the retrieval process requiring hospitalization
- Internal bleeding as a result of the retrieval process requiring hospitalization

If an agency does not provide facilitation between you and an insurance company, it would be your responsibility to make sure that a policy is taken out. Most insurance companies now have an easily accessible online application that you can fill out for your donor, usually by donor's first name and a patient number (either provided by your agency or doctor's office). You would then provide a credit card for the policy payment and the start date of her medications. The policies typically last from day one of medication through four months.

On average, the insurance policies cost between $250 and $500. A higher policy limit, which would have a higher premium, could be purchased by the intended parents as well. Additionally, you can add intended mothers onto the policy, which would cover her for complications resulting from medications or transfer complications.

Occasionally, there will be a complication that is a direct result of the egg donation process but is not covered by insurance. Most agencies now have an addendum added to their contracts stating that noninsurance covered complications would be the responsibility of the intended parents up to $2,500. Kate Lyon, a member of the CA State Bar, practicing in Los Angeles who specializes in reproductive law, explains why this addition is necessary:

> The clause regarding coverage for uncovered expenses (to a maximum of $2,500) is a reasonable assumption of risk for the intended parents, as well as for the donor. The intended parents will not have to pay more than $2,500 in uncovered expenses that might occur, but the donor will not be out-of-pocket for medical costs associated with the retrieval process up to the cap of $2,500. She assumes the risk of anything beyond that (which is rare, but not unheard of).

> With this type of clause, we are protecting the donor against the cost of uncovered medical expenses for complications related to the retrieval process or procedures (meaning, it could be complications from medication or complications from the retrieval itself). This type of clause is becoming the industry standard.

> The likelihood of the donor having any uncovered expenses is small, but in my years of practice, I have had a handful of donors that had to battle with the insurance company to cover expenses that the clinic supported as costs associated with the cycle. Without such a clause as we are requesting, the donor is forced to utilize her own

donor fee to cover the expenses. Not to mention the time and effort it takes to work with the insurance company, the agency, etc., long after the cycle is over, to sort these issues out.

The reality is that despite the appearance of adding an additional fee to an already expensive process, the risk to the intended parents is small. The insurance policies are very comprehensive, so this type of clause is really added to protect against a totally unforeseen circumstance. Such a clause protects the donor to a certain degree, and then she agrees to assume the remainder of risk.

Most egg donor agencies will act as facilitators between intended parents and the insurance company on when and where to go to take out your egg donor's policy. We would be wary of any agency that does not require you to take out a policy on your donor or leaves it to you to make sure this policy is in place. If an agency says that the donor will be responsible for any complications as a result of the cycle with her own insurance, this is incorrect and could potentially lead to a very unfortunate situation. Should the donor end up being hospitalized for hyperstimulation, for example, and her bill ends up being $15,000—not only will her primary insurance (should she even have it) not cover this, but she should also not be responsible for this payment regardless. Should the donor come back to collect this money from her intended parents, the law would most likely side on behalf of the donor. Therefore, a low cost insurance policy is a far better situation for all involved.

LEGAL CONTRACTS

We gave you some great insights from Steven Lazarus on the importance of contracts in Chapter 6. However, whether you're from the United States or traveling to the states from abroad, it's important to make sure that a valid legal document, drawn up by a board-certified attorney, is signed and initialed by both you and your egg donor. The American Academy of Assisted Reproductive Technology Attorneys (AAARTA) will provide a list of attorneys in your area who specialize in this field. You can also ask your egg donor agency or IVF clinic which attorneys they recommend based on their personal experience or client reviews. This contract should be reviewed and signed by all parties preferably prior to injection medication start date, but it absolutely needs to be completed before the retrieval takes place. Many IVF clinics will not allow a cycle to start or even create a cycle calendar until legal contracts are signed by all parties. Paperwork, paperwork, paperwork; but don't overlook the importance in making sure all parties who are coming together to assist in this process have the appropriate legal protections.

HORMONE TESTING

As your donor enters her cycle, she'll undergo some hormone testing. The most common type of hormone testing performed on egg donors was discussed previously in Chapter 6 and include FSH, E2, AFC and sometimes AMH, inhibin B, and chlomid challenge. Because the accuracy of the tests are based on an administration date of Day 2 or 3 of her menstrual cycle, she will likely go in at the time of her next period after being chosen as a donor. These tests generally end up coinciding with her genetic and psychological evaluations.

FDA AND CLINIC-REQUIRED MEDICAL SCREENING

In addition to the testing required by the FDA, each clinic may also have their own set of required tests that all egg donors must take. The FDA requires that your donor undergo a complete physical examination; testing for HIV, HTLV and hepatitis, and sexually transmitted diseases (including syphilis, gonorrhea, and chlamydia); and screening for illicit/controlled drug use.

In addition to the screening mentioned, modern medical technology makes it easy to screen for many genetic traits via various tests. Most donors today are screened for cystic fibrosis, spinal muscular atrophy, fragile X, and other tests depending on ethnicity. Donors of Asian, Mediterranean, and African descent should undergo a hemoglobin electrophoresis as screen for thalassemias and sickle cell trait. If the donor is of Ashkenazi Jewish origin, screening for Tay-Sachs disease, Canavan disease, and Gaucher disease is indicated. Donors of French-Canadian descent should also be screened for Tay-Sachs disease. Additional genetic testing and karyotyping of the donor may be offered by some programs or requested by the recipient.

If your donor undergoes genetic counseling and the report suggests additional tests based on her family genetic history, it is important to schedule a time to discuss this with your doctor prior to your donor's initial medical screening. Some doctors will require any tests suggested as a result of a genetic report, whereas others will simply keep the report in the chart and do no additional testing. Although it would be nice for all medical facilities to dot every *i* and cross every *t*, it is not something you should conditionally count on. Because genetic testing is not an FDA requirement and the cost of additional testing is generally not covered in the medical screening fees, many clinics will just ignore these suggestions unless you specifically inquire about having them performed. This isn't meant to frighten you, as more often than not the donor ends up testing as a noncarrier. However, it should be *your* choice to pay for additional testing should the need arise.

Medical screening tests generally take about 10–14 days to get results back. There may be situations that arise where your donor will have a test result that requires additional information. This may necessitate her taking another test. Results can also indicate that she is a carrier for something that is not of significant risk to your offspring so long as the other half of the genetic equation, or the sperm donor/intended father, is not affected.

During this testing process, your physician will most likely be working on building your cycle calendar so he or she can have it ready to go once all of the required results are back and favorable.

CALENDAR DATES AND MEDICATION

Is it time? Yes, it's time! Once the intended parent(s), surrogate (if using one), and your egg donor have been medically cleared, you'll receive your cycle dates. This includes suppression phase, stimulation, retrieval, fertilization, and anticipated transfer dates for all parties.

Calendars

Calendars for donors and intended mothers/surrogates will generally have listed

- appointment dates
- medication start dates
- dosage, type, and dates for all medications
- estimated dates for egg retrieval and embryo transfer

Dosages, types of drugs, screening tests, and a number of required appointments will vary from clinic to clinic. Your physician will take into consideration the expected response of your donor based on age, initial hormone test results, previous cycle outcomes or a number of other variables.

TRAVEL COORDINATION

If you've selected a donor who resides out of your area, there will be some coordination involved for both her monitoring and her ultimate travel to your facility for the retrieval procedure. Your fertility clinic and egg donor agency will handle these coordination efforts, and here are the things they'll be working on as your donor begins her cycle:

Monitoring Facility Coordination

To expand on what we covered in Chapter 6, selecting an out-of-area donor requires the use of a monitoring facility near your egg donor's hometown that will perform all of her in-cycle monitoring throughout the process. They'll handle everything from ultrasounds to blood tests and make sure your physician receives the results, usually the same day.

How will your home IVF clinic locate a qualified monitoring facility for your donor? SART has a list of all registered IVF clinics across the United States, so it's easy for your IVF clinic to obtain information on facilities outside their area.

Travel

We'll expand on the potential travel expenses for out-of-area donors covered in Chapter 6. For most out-of-area donors, there will be two trips to your IVF clinic—one at the beginning of her cycle for her initial screening and one at the end for the retrieval. Whereas the initial trip will be, most likely, a day trip or one with a single overnight stay, the second trip for the retrieval will be between 5 and 10 days on average, including the retrieval procedure. Because of the sensitive nature of the egg donation process, your physician will want to be the one who sees your donor for her last few appointments prior to her hCG trigger shot.

MEDICATIONS

We all know it takes a little helping hand from medical science to create your family, but what kinds of helping hands can you expect to encounter in your egg donor IVF cycle? There are common medications used throughout most egg donation cycles, and those are the ones that will receive our focus. Ultimately, your physician will decide which medications are best for you and your donor to take during the course of the cycle, and this will always reflect your personal medical history as well as your IVF clinic's standard protocols.

We've worked with David Tourgeman, MD, and Bradford Kolb, MD, from Huntington Reproductive Center to compile the following list of potential medications that you and your egg donor might be prescribed during the course of a typical cycle.

Suppression Hormones

Suppression hormones are used to prevent premature ovulation or ovulation that would normally occur during your donor's menstrual cycle. Stimulation of the pituitary gland in the brain produces a luteinizing hormone (LH) and follicle-stimulating hormone (FSH) that together cause ovulation. By suppressing the pituitary gland, your physician will then be able to create an environment for stimulating more follicles in her ovaries during the artificial IVF procedure than would naturally be matured. The most common suppression medications are the following:

- Leuprolide acetate (Lupron)—taken by subcutaneous injection
- Ganirelix (Antagon)—taken by subcutaneous injection
- Cetrotide—taken by subcutaneous injection
- Nafarelin acetate (Synarel)—taken in the form of a nasal spray

Common side effects to suppression medications include

- hot flashes or night sweats
- mild headaches
- drowsiness
- insomnia
- oily skin and/or acne
- bruising at injection site

Follicle-Stimulating Hormones (FSH)

FSH hormones are used to stimulate the growth of multiple immature follicles in the ovaries. Egg donors are prescribed a specific amount of FSH hormones to stimulate the follicles to mature. The ideal goal (which will vary per IVF clinic) is generally accepted as being between 10 and 20 mature follicles at the end of a stimulation cycle prior to retrieval.

The most common FSH medications are the following:

- Follistim—usually taken via subcutaneous injection
- Gonal-f—usually taken via subcutaneous injection
- Bravelle—usually taken via subcutaneous injection
- Menopur—combined FSH and LH hormone, taken via subcutaneous or intramuscular injection

Common or possible side effects to taking FSH medications include the following:

- Ovarian enlargement, bloating, OHSS (see following section on Potential Complications)
- Fatigue
- Tender breasts
- Mood swings
- Bruising and/or temporary pain at injection site
- Infection (from needles used for injecting medications)
- Increased risk for pregnancy

Human Chorionic Gonadotrophin (hCG)

Human chorionic gonadotrophin (hCG) is a hormone that stimulates the eggs to mature and detach from the wall of the follicle so it can be recovered during the egg retrieval procedure. Some clinics will have the donor come into the office on the day prior to the egg retrieval to confirm that the donor took her hCG. This can be detected in a urine or blood pregnancy test.

Additional Medications That May Be Taken

As every egg donor, IVF cycle has its nuances; we've put together a list of additional medications you might find as a part of your or your donor's prescribed protocol.

- Birth control pills—used to synchronize the menstrual cycle of the recipient and donor
- Progesterone/estrogen—given to the intended mother or surrogate to prepare the uterus for the embryo transfer. These hormones are necessary to achieve and sustain a pregnancy in the first trimester
- Anticoagulants—such as baby aspirin, may increase blood flow to the uterus or increase the chances of implantation
- Antibiotics—often prescribed to egg donors starting a few of days prior to retrieval to lessen the risk of potential infection during or after the retrieval procedure
- Steroids—used as an anti-inflammatory agent, thought to help the embryo implant into the uterus of the intended mother or surrogate

The medications listed are the most common, but not the only ones used during an egg donation cycle. If your doctor is using a different medication, it does not mean that the cycle will be in any way compromised because most doctors use variations of the same types of medications. You are always encouraged to ask as many questions that makes you feel comfortable regarding your particular physician's choices and reasons behind them. This is your journey, and there's no shame in asking for as many answers as you need to feel comfortable with the process.

THE CYCLE PROCESS

Once your donor has her calendar and the dates to start her medications, the process generally follows a fairly predictable time frame. We consulted with Bradford Kolb, MD, of Huntington Reproductive Center to help lay out the details.

Lupron Instruction: One to two days prior to your donor's initial Lupron injection, the doctor's office or monitoring facility will usually have your donor go in for an injection lesson. This usually includes a donor giving herself a demonstration injection and/or watching the nurse do one. The clinic will then confirm that the donor knows how to give herself the injection and how much medication to give.

Some clinics choose to give injection lessons via an instruction manual with photos and step-by-step explanations. Other facilities have online instructional videos that the donor can go watch that explains and demonstrates how the injections are given.

Additionally, some pharmaceutical companies such as Freedom Pharmacy, EMD Serono, and Merck have instructions online for all types of medications.

Stimulation Start: Once a donor has been on Lupron for approximately 10–15 days, she will have a blood test to determine if she is suppressed enough to continue on to the stimulation process. The clinic will also perform a vaginal ultrasound to confirm appropriate suppression and that there are no cysts in her ovaries that may complicate the cycle. Similarly to her Lupron instructions, she will be given a lesson on how to administer her stimulation injections.

Regular Appointments: Once your donor has been on her stimulation injections for approximately four days, she will begin having regular appointments at your physician's office or monitoring facility (if an out-of-area donor) to check her estrogen levels and follicular growth. What is your medical team looking for? The follicles should be growing at a regular rate and increasing in size at each appointment.

Your fertility specialist may change the dosage of stimulation medications depending on how your donor is progressing.

Trigger Shot (HCG, Ovidrel, or Lupron): Once the follicles are between 18 and 20 mm with at least two follicles greater than 18 mm, the trigger shot is administered. The trigger shot will stimulate the eggs to complete their maturation and release from the walls of the follicle into the follicular fluid so the eggs can be collected at the time of retrieval. This shot is typically administered on a very strict schedule of 36 hours prior to the retrieval procedure.

Retrieval: The retrieval process will take place approximately 36 hours after the trigger shot. The physician's office will supply adequate sedation or anesthesia (total conscious sedation) so that her eggs can be safely and comfortably retrieved. Your donor will be able to breathe on her own as no intubation is required with this type of anesthesia.

The retrieval is performed via a process called transvaginal aspiration. This entails inserting a thin needle, under ultrasound guidance, through the vaginal wall and into the ovaries. The follicular fluid and eggs are aspirated into a test tube. The fluid is then inspected by the embryologist, who separates the eggs from the fluid. The eggs are then assessed for maturity, and the most viable are fertilized. The retrieval process takes approximately 20 minutes, and the donor is often awake again 30–60 minutes later.

Your donor will be required to have a friend, relative, or domestic care service take her to and from her retrieval because she will not be able to drive due to the anesthesia. Your agency should follow up with your donor to confirm she has someone to be there for her or arrange for a service to provide this if necessary.

POSSIBLE COMPLICATIONS

Most doctors we've spoken to regarding the safety of the egg donation and retrieval process all state that they would feel safe if their own daughters chose to be an egg donor so long as they understood the risks and processes involved. As with any medical procedure, however, there are some potential complications associated with the retrieval process. If you've been through an IVF cycle before, you've no doubt heard of these. We'll review them so you know what both you and your donor could potentially experience.

Ovarian Hyperstimulation Syndrome (OHSS)

OHSS is the most common complication experienced by egg donors. Most donors only experience mild hyperstimulation, although on rare occasions, she may experience serious complications. OHSS happens after the hCG trigger shot and retrieval has occurred, although there may be some signs prior to the retrieval based on the number of follicles that are stimulating in the ovaries and how high the estrogen levels become. Higher follicle count and estrogen levels are indicators of possible OHSS. Severe hyperstimulation is characterized by pelvic pain, nausea, vomiting, shortness of breath, water retention that leads to weight gain and abdominal bloating, and decreased urine output. These symptoms are caused by enlargement of the ovaries after egg retrieval and present as fluid retention in the abdomen and in the soft tissues of the body.

In cases of mild to moderate OHSS, donors are instructed to stay hydrated, increase electrolyte intake, and limit any strenuous activity. In more severe cases, the donor my require IV hydration and removal of excess fluid from the abdomen at the clinic via an outpatient procedure. In severe cases, as characterized by the donor's inability to maintain hydration, lack of urination, or extreme pelvic pain, hospitalization might be required. Hospitalization allows for continuous IV hydration, monitoring electrolytes, management of the donor's pain, and in some cases removal of excess fluids from the abdomen. If hospitalization is required, it is typically only for a limited time.

Infection

Infections are rare but always a risk when a procedure involves the use of injections or needles. To prevent infection during and after the retrieval process, egg donors are typically prescribed antibiotics to take starting two to three days prior to their scheduled procedure and to continue two to five days following. Most egg donors are also given antibiotics in their IV by the anesthesiologist during the retrieval process or in recovery. Signs of infection include vomiting, nausea, fever, pain, swelling, vaginal discharge, and heat at or near an injection site.

Torsion

This is a rare side effect, but ovaries often swell during the egg donation process, putting an egg donor at higher risk of ovarian torsion. In torsion, the ovary rotates or twists on its axis, resulting in the blood flow from the ovarian vein or artery to be cut off. In rare instances, significant loss of blood flow could cause permanent damage or infarction of the ovary, potentially resulting in the need for removal. Most common symptoms include moderate-to-severe abdominal pain and vomiting.

Anesthesia

All types of anesthesia involve some risk, though the chances are slim that there will be any adverse effects. There will be an anesthesiologist present to monitor your egg donor throughout the retrieval process, and she will be able to breathe on her own because the mild anesthesia used for retrieval procedures does not require intubation. Common side effects include nausea, vomiting, and grogginess. In rare cases, breathing, heart rate, blood pressure, and other bodily functions may be affected.

Internal Bleeding

Although rare, there have been some reported cases of internal bleeding when the needle damages blood vessels or the bowel during the retrieval procedure. In the rare cases, this bleeding can lead to hemorrhaging. Symptoms would include excessive bleeding, abdominal pain, and fever; and hospitalization might be necessary to resolve the bleeding and stabilize the donor.

Reactions to Antibiotics

Possible allergic reactions to antibiotics require affected egg donors to be put on a different prescription. In rare cases, the allergic reaction may be severe.

Possible Long-Term Side Effects

Some older studies had suggested that patients taking fertility medications were at an increased risk for breast or ovarian cancer. Many of these studies were poorly controlled. A majority of subsequent studies following good scientific standards does not make this association. Currently, most fertility experts do not feel that there are long-term consequences to taking fertility medications.

CYCLE EXPECTATIONS

Now that your donor has cycled, your embryos are maturing, and you're preparing for retrieval, it's common to ask, "Has my cycle been one that's considered *normal?*" Hopefully your fertility specialist has reviewed with you prior to beginning your cycle what can be considered a normal result with most egg donors they've worked with, but just in case and perhaps as a review, we'll review the range of "normal" here.

The average number of eggs retrieved from the typical egg donor cycle is between 10 and 20. In some cases, donors have more than 20 eggs, but this is outside of the norm. A recent study quoted 15 eggs as the "magic" number for the best chance of a cycle to result in a live birth.[10] A report from *Human Reproduction Journal* in the United Kingdom analyzed more than 400,000 IVF cycles conducted between 1991 and 2008, demonstrating an association between the number of eggs retrieved in an IVF cycle and subsequent live birth rates.[11] Let's explore what that means for your egg donor cycle.

Let's say you start out with 15 eggs—of these eggs retrieved, there is the possibility that not all of them will be mature enough to fertilize properly. Of the mature eggs that fertilize, not all of them are likely to become viable embryos. The best thing to do is to ask your fertility clinic for their fertilization rates so you have a sound range of expectations for your own cycle. If they list fertilization rates at 70%–80%, then you will likely end up with 10–12 fertilized embryos from a donor cycle that netted you 15 eggs. If you take these embryos to the blast stage or perform PGD on them, then there is a likely chance that you will end up with less than 10–12 because of the attrition rates attached to each of these protocols, but the resulting embryos could arguably be of much higher quality.

Ultimately, an ideal cycle will result in both a fresh and frozen cycle transfer opportunity. This means that even if you end up with only four blastocyst embryos, one or two can be used for the fresh cycle transfer and two or three frozen for later use.

OUTCOME

It's the day you've been waiting for—when you as the intended mother or your surrogate receive the embryo transfer. An embryo transfer, which includes putting one or more embryos into the recipient mother's or surrogate's uterus, usually takes place within 3–6 days following retrieval. At this point, you should have come to an agreement with your physician on how many embryos to transfer and the reasoning behind their recommendations. Depending on the outcome of the retrieval and fertilization, this decision can, of course, be adjusted to optimize results. For example, if you originally decided to transfer only two embryos but end up with three embryos total from the fertilization process (and one of which is of questionable quality), your physician may suggest transferring all three because the third embryo would likely not survive the freezing and unfreezing process for a future transfer. Ultimately, the decision as to how many embryos to transfer is yours as the recipient, but understand that your physician will make the best recommendations possible for your particular scenario and in the interests of ethics alike.

Approximately 10–12 days after embryo transfer, a blood test is performed to determine if the transfer resulted in a pregnancy. We won't try to mask the reality of this "waiting period" because it's probably going to send most of the intended parents reading this book through a litany of emotional challenges that will range from extremely excited and hopeful to nervous and fearing the worst. We'll tell you to relax, as if you're the one who received the transfer; a relaxed state can only help improve your chances of achieving pregnancy. We know, however, the emotional turmoil of the waiting game. This is a good time to find ways to pamper yourself and adhere to your physician's guidelines for posttransfer rest. Catch up on your reading, reconnect with friends and loved ones, and most importantly, love yourself! Being cautiously optimistic in the wake of a trying journey is most intended parents allow themselves to feel at this point. So many times, we lose out on some incredible moments to celebrate and feel joy and hope in fear of future disappointment. If the latter is going to happen, it will happen whether you celebrate or not—so allow yourself this moment and just go for it.

And multiples? We should all be so lucky! Although we know you're hoping for simply a positive pregnancy test, you should definitely have the discussion with your physician (and partner, if applicable) about the implications of a multiples pregnancy if you transferred more than one embryo. Review the options for selective reduction, your feelings about the procedure, and your access to OB/GYNs who specialize in high-risk pregnancies. Your fertility specialist will certainly have a list of recommendations, which is great information to have on hand should the need arise.

UPS AND DOWNS

If you discover that the transfer didn't result in a pregnancy, now is the time to seek out those people in your life who can provide you with the support you need—as you need it now. From your donor agency to your fertility counselor to friends, family, and spouses, there's love waiting for you all around. Take the time you need and determine how you'll move forward with your options for building your family. We hope it's reassuring to share that, over the years, Erika has donated for intended mothers who didn't achieve pregnancy on the first transfer, but the next proved to be a charm. Wendie has worked with many intended parents who cycled more than once to realize their dream. Your situation is yours and yours alone and with the help of multiple professionals who are dedicated to helping you through the ups and downs of family building in your corner, we hope you'll find a way to enjoy the journey, laugh when life tells you to do otherwise, and celebrate in the small victories in hopes there will be the biggest victory of all waiting for you down the road.

Key Chapter Highlights—Circling the Nest—The Ovum Donation Cycle

- Understand that medical protocols will vary between every IVF clinic.

- Understand all of the responsibilities that you and your egg donor agency share to ensure a smooth cycle (such as insurance, legal contracts, etc.).

- Be sure to discuss with your physician not only the expectations for your protocol, but your donor's as well.

8

Readying the Nest:
Transfer and Beyond

The long-awaited day for your embryo transfer has arrived! It doesn't matter if it's you or your surrogate—what happens next is going to require a fair amount of patience. Throughout the egg donor cycle process, you've surrounded yourself with a team of professionals who are dedicated to helping you achieve your ideal goal. Awaiting a pregnancy result is perhaps the most challenging part of the egg donor cycle process, so we'll tell you that our best advice is to

- listen to your physician
- get plenty of rest
- keep your stress levels at a minimum
- have hope!

As you take a deep breath and enter this next stage of your egg donor journey, we'll go over some of the most common scenarios intended parents face, including making the transition from your fertility specialist to an OB/GYN for the duration of your pregnancy, the chance for multiples, selective reduction, frozen embryo cycles, negative pregnancy results, and emotional considerations for those who need to prepare for the next stage of their journey. We're fortunate to have insights from Abigail Glass, MFT, and Eric Scott Sills, MD, contributing to the information that follows—their contributions are an invaluable part of building you the most comprehensive resource for egg donation possible.

POSITIVE PREGNANCY: MAKING THE TRANSITION
FROM PATIENT TO PARENT (ERIC SCOTT SILLS, MD)

In most IVF programs, objective evidence confirming a viable intrauterine pregnancy can be obtained at around Day 60. Understandably, this "first

111

pregnancy ultrasound" is an important event for everyone concerned. It is at this stage that the pregnancy may be classified as singleton, twin gestation, and so forth. Several reports have concluded that measurement of the embryonic heart rate can correlate with the risk of a subsequent miscarriage, so this is usually documented along with other features at the time of the scan. No studies have determined exactly how many ultrasound scans need to be done in early pregnancy, but at least one scan should be completed under the direction of the IVF clinic before the intended parent or gestational surrogate transitions to an OB/GYN for prenatal care. When does this "graduation" occur? Typically around 8 to 10 weeks gestational age mark. Remember, your OB/GYN team will want to make you a part of their practice in a timely fashion, so the IVF clinic facilitates a seamless transfer to make this possible. At our practice in Orange County, a summary letter is sent to the OB/GYN providing the results of the treatment (a success!) and details about the pregnancy—including estimated due date.

Regrettably, there really is no formal mechanism for IVF clinics to stay in the loop after this. Once the "pre-OB" experience has concluded at the IVF clinic, we want our patients to have an unremarkable pregnancy course in the hands of our OB/GYN colleagues. Particularly for patients who live far from our clinic, the arrival of a birth announcement and photo kindly mailed in from the new family nine months later is our only way to know the ultimately happy outcome.

SELECTIVE REDUCTION AND MULTIPLE GESTATION (ABIGAIL GLASS, MFT, AND WENDIE WILSON-MILLER)

It's not uncommon for intended parents to achieve multiple gestation, especially if more than one embryo is transferred. Whether you're the one carrying the pregnancy or you're working with a surrogate, it's advisable to discuss both multiple pregnancy and selective reduction with both your fertility specialist and your therapist prior to transfer so you're mentally prepared for the decisions that go along with these scenarios. I'll review the implications for both, as multiples are both a tremendous joy and a potential risk, depending on your personal medical profile.

Selective Reduction

In a perfect world, I get to work with intended parents prior to embryo transfer to cover the potential need for selective reduction; a difficult decision that occasionally goes hand in hand with the transfer of multiple embryos. Quite often, there are two people whose emotions need to be taken into consideration, and counseling helps both intended parents voice their feelings so they can come to an acceptable conclusion that leaves them both feeling confident in moving forward.

Although it is not often discussed, I think it's important to explain to intended parents exactly what's involved in the selective reduction process. So often recipient parents are blindsided by the joy of a pregnancy that the advisement that they could be at-risk due to multiples is a shock. It is better to address the issue at the forefront than having to make a decision under duress.

Intended parents choose to selectively reduce for many reasons; from concern for the intended mother's or surrogate's health, the health of the children, and even the fear of becoming a parent to more than one child at a time. Without a doubt, reduction is a huge decision to face, especially when also faced with achieving your family goal. Many people have both spiritual and personal roads they must travel to be able to make the best decision. Sure, there are some intended parents who have no problem accepting selective reduction as a very real possibility, and others have strong beliefs to the contrary. Whatever your position is, it's yours and yours alone. I advise you to take to heart the advice of your fertility specialist, especially if he or she conveys a significant health risk attached to not selectively reducing. This is a topic with a great deal of emotional, spiritual, and practical implications attached to it, and the best thing you can do is understand all sides of the issue so you can own whatever decision, if any, you must make.

This is a time in your journey where you need to feel free to make the best choice for you and not be judged by others. There are often so many things going on during a typical egg donation and IVF cycle that this issue is accidentally missed. I have had many people throughout the years forced to make a difficult decision when they found out they were pregnant with multiples following the transfer of two or three embryos. This, unfortunately, is one of the many unexpected situations that can arise even after the joy of a positive pregnancy test. The best thing to do for your emotional journey is to be fully prepared and bring up the issue with both your physician and therapist prior to the time where a decision must be made.

Multiples Pregnancy

You've dreamed of a family for so long, so what do you do when faced with the reality of having not just one, but two—possibly three—children all at one go? For some multiples are a blessing in disguise and for others a source of very real concern and possibly panic. Let's discuss some of the practical and emotional issues of multiples so you know where to start your own conversation with both your fertility practitioner and partner, if applicable.

Practically, multiple pregnancies are most always classified as high risk. You or your surrogate could be on longer bed rest, are at risk for early delivery, and will certainly be more highly monitored by your OB/GYN throughout your pregnancy term. It's a good conversation to have up-front with your surrogate, if applicable, to ensure that if a multiples pregnancy is achieved—and if she's agreeable to carrying more than one child—what additional compensation must be paid for this privilege. If you've reached the point of using an egg donor to build your family, it's unlikely you haven't come across the possibility and implications of multiples prior to now. Yet it's still sound to review a few important details to consider if you're with a multiple pregnancy.

Pregnancy and Birth

- High-risk pregnancy
- Premature birth
- Potential health risk to babies during the gestational period

At Home

- Extra help and support
- Two (or more) of everything (diapers, strollers, etc.)!
- Breast milk or formula considerations
- Financial reserves (costs are higher with multiple children)

Conversely, if you feel strongly that you could not handle the pregnancy or the cost, time, and so forth that it takes to raise a bigger family, you will need to discuss an extremely limited embryo transfer approach with your physician before moving ahead. Multiples might seem like a dream, and families all over the world are raising twins and triplets, but the ideal scenario is the ideal one for *you*, not anyone else.

FROZEN EMBRYOS AND FUTURE CYCLES (ERIC SCOTT SILLS, MD)

The science of cryobiology has advanced significantly over the past few decades. Most patients want to have any nontransferred (i.e., surplus) embryos placed in frozen storage for possible future use. If the fresh cycle does not result in a pregnancy and frozen embryos are available, then a frozen embryo transfer (FET) cycle can usually be arranged much more easily than starting over from the very beginning. Accordingly, the cost for FET is generally much lower compared to a de novo (fresh) IVF cycle. Nearly all IVF programs by now will have an embryo freezing program, and it may be helpful to ask your particular physician about the post-thaw viability rate at your center. A survival rate that is consistently less than 75% may raise some concerns unless there are special factors to explain it.

Several ways have been described to accomplish freezing, although there is debate among experts about which method is best. If your fresh embryo transfer is successful and you have frozen embryos in storage and want to grow your family after a period of time, then FET can be scheduled to accomplish this. Remember, human embryos that are frozen at $-196°C$ are essentially metabolically inactive, therefore they do not age like other normal cells. No one knows exactly how long the *shelf life* might be for a frozen human embryo from IVF, but it may be hundreds of years!

NEGATIVE PREGNANCY RESULTS AND NEXT STEPS (ABIGAIL GLASS, MFT, WENDIE WILSON-MILLER, AND ERIKA NAPOLETANO)

No matter if you're trying to achieve pregnancy the old-fashioned way or using every advantage known to medical technology, you're hoping for a positive outcome. You wouldn't be going through all of this if you didn't have *some* hope that it would all work out and bring you your family, right? The reality of the situation is that many of you going through egg donation won't achieve pregnancy on your first or perhaps even several subsequent transfers. So how do you take the news that your cycle didn't result in your much hoped for pregnancy?

We have spoken time and time again of the support structure that you've built up through your egg donation process, composed of professionals ready to help you every step of the way. A negative pregnancy result is no different. Your doctor's and egg donor agency's hearts will all break right alongside yours, and with that heartbreak will come a supporting embrace that's ready to carry you into your next steps. Although every intended parent manages the news of a negative pregnancy result in different ways, we've found that it's helpful for you to reach out and let the people who are trained to help you help. Your therapist? At the ready. Your egg donor agency? Ready to explore solutions and alternatives. Your fertility specialist? Analyzing results and offering advice for the next chance for success.

Although no intended parent wants to plan for a negative pregnancy result and wants to keep a positive outlook, planning for adverse results is a practice that can save you a certain amount of heartache if that time should come. Have you discussed what you/you and your partner will do if this cycle doesn't work? Are you going to give yourself a month to process and then reevaluate? Are you going to consider a different path? Are there other paths you might choose to pursue, such as adoption, should this cycle not result in a pregnancy? These are questions that might not have obvious answers when you first begin to consider them, but allow yourself (and your partner, if applicable) time to ponder the possible answers and arrive at ones where you feel comfortable.

We've also found that it's especially helpful for intended parents to plan for the day when they'll receive the results of their pregnancy test. Be sure to have yourself in a place where you are supported and can have whatever reaction arises. Plan to have the people with you that will feel good to you. Don't get the call while you are at your desk at work. Place yourself in a position where you're at the height of environmental and emotional comfort, and you'll be better able to handle whatever information comes through your phone lines!

RESOURCES FOR MANAGING YOUR POST-TRANSFER EGG DONATION JOURNEY

The following is a list of suggestions and resources to help you through whatever the next stage in your journey might be. From psychological professionals to support groups and coping techniques, we hope you'll find it to be a list on which not only can you rely, but also one that has techniques that you can carry with you throughout your life to help with any challenging situation.

- **Find a therapist who specializes in ART families:** ASRM has a list of therapists who specialize in infertility counseling. You can also find your local chapter of RESOLVE (www.resolve.org). Parents Via Egg Donation (www.pved.org) will also be able to help you find a therapist, or you'll be able to connect with other intended parents and ask for referrals. Also, your agency and IVF clinic will usually have a list of therapists they've previously worked with that come highly recommended.

- **Social support system:** Your egg donation journey is going to require you to have someone you can lean on during the difficult times. Plan ahead about whom you are going to tell about using an egg donor. Make sure to take into consideration the personality type of those you are going to share this information with. This is not the time to choose someone who has a tendency to be judgmental or who will experience difficulty maintaining your privacy. The last thing you want during this process is to have to work at considering how other people feel about your journey especially those who you haven't chosen to share the information with. This is your (or you and your partner's) very personal experience. Whoever you share this with needs to be someone who can deeply and compassionately respect that.

- **Write a letter:** Many people find letter writing to be extremely therapeutic. It can help you grieve the loss of your own eggs and cope with miscarriages, selective reduction decisions, or a negative pregnancy test. It can also aid in accepting and welcoming the donor's eggs into your life. Here are some suggestions to get you started:

- Mourning the loss of your eggs: "Dear eggs, I am very sad that I am not able to use you in my body to have a baby . . . "

- Miscarriage: "Dear baby, I was so hopeful that you were going to continue growing in my belly and join us in this life . . . "

- Selective reduction: "Dear embryo, I am very sad that I have to let you go . . . "

- To donor eggs: "Dear eggs, Thank you for joining me and my body (or surrogate's body) to help us have a family . . . "

- **Mantras for strength, positivity, and coping:** Mantras are a positive way to help your subconscious mind change negative thinking patterns. Put in the first person present tense as what you want to be feeling or experiencing in that moment. For those who want help with creating a positive outlook, here are some suggestions, but you should feel free to modify or build your own mantras based on what you would like to manifest in your life at any given time. We've included some visualization aids along with the verbal mantras for those who work better with visual cues.

- **I am at peace and relaxed.** (Imagine yourself next to a quiet lake, the sun coming through the trees, and the sound of a soft breeze rustling the leaves.)

- **I have good feelings for myself and others.** (Imagine yourself surrounded by close friends, family, and loved ones. Feel a sense of happiness, peace, and love radiating through all of you.)

- **I am strong!** (You can use something you associate with strength, such as an ocean or a mountain, i.e., repeat "I am an ocean" while visualizing yourself as strong waves crashing on the shore, or "I am a mountain" while you look out at the world below you or the sky above you.)

- **I am in control.**

- **I am able to rise above this.** (Imagine yourself as a bird soaring over the world below.)

- **I am a mother/father.** (Imagine yourself holding your baby, smelling their hair, and rocking them to sleep.)

- **Take care of your health**: It is no secret that good health is important, if not fundamental, to your fertility (whether male or female). To be a fully functioning human being on all levels, we need to be both physically and mentally healthy. Eating a diet rich with fresh fruits and vegetables, whole grains, and lean proteins will significantly aid in handling the hormones involved in IVF cycles and pregnancy, as well as help manage the stress that comes along with it. Doing good things for your body does good things for your mind. Don't neglect the *one person* who needs as much TLC as they can get during this journey, and that's *you*.

- **Have a "what's next" plan**: Because this is an imperfect process, you always need to be emotionally prepared to handle any outcome. Although it is true that most of egg donors' cycles move forward without incident, there are many things that can happen to cause another bump in your road. The reality is that these things happen and when they do, it is normal and expected that you will be disappointed. What we want to avoid is having you become so emotionally devastated that you are unable to contemplate what's next. Here are some suggestions for building your "what's next" plan:

  - **Have a second donor in mind** in case the first one doesn't work out. You may even realize that the one you ultimately cycle with is the one you connect with more anyway.

  - **Budget wisely.** If a cycle doesn't work and you have exceeded your financial limit, you may decide to take a break for a few months and get back on track (emotionally and financially). Decide on a time frame to pick back up again. Decide this in advance of your cycle and honor it, regardless of your emotional response in the event of a negative pregnancy result.

  - **Plan to take a vacation and relax.** Have something to look forward to!

  - **Prepare your social support system or therapist**, telling them that you will need extra support during this time.

  - **Talk about how long you are willing to try** one avenue before pursuing another (i.e., adoption, fostering, letting go, etc.).

- **Breathing techniques.** One thing everybody needs to be reminded of from time to time is to just *breathe*. Take just a few minutes out of each day to concentrate on your breathing, and you'll notice a significant difference in your ability to handle anything that comes your way. Here are a few suggestions based on what was shared with us by yoga instructor Terren Burson; these which have always brought practitioners back to their breath as a constant source of strength and support.

Day-to-Day

- Sit comfortably with a tall, straight spine. The shoulders should be stacked over the hips, ears over the shoulders. You can also close your eyes if you prefer.
- Place one palm over the center of your heart and the other over your low belly right below the navel.
- As you *inhale*, first breathe into your top hand and feel your chest rise and ribs expand, continue the breath down the body to fill up your belly and allow the belly to expand into your lower hand. Inhale to six counts (or more if you can).
- As you *exhale*, let the air out of your belly first and then your chest. Exhale out to six (or the same count as you inhaled).

Tip: For healthy day-to-day breathing, keep inhales and exhales long, deep, and even in length. You should be breathing all the way down to your belly. Let your inhales lift you higher and your exhales soften and relax the mind and body. If your entire torso does not move when you breathe, then you are not breathing deeply enough.

Stress Relieving

You can sit or lay down for this variation, just make sure that you can relax and breathe comfortably.

- Inhale through your nose for four counts and breathe to fill up your belly.
- Exhale through the mouth for six counts and let the body relax as the breath leaves the body.
- Continue this count repetition or gradually increase but always make your exhale at least two beats longer than the inhale.
- Repeat five to ten times.
- Now, close the mouth and inhale and exhale through your nose.

Tip: When breathing to relieve the mind and body of stress and anxiety, it is important to emphasize the exhalations and let the exhales soften the body of the physical manifestations of stress (i.e., tight muscles, tight joints, etc.).

Energizing Breath

- Sit tall and in a comfortable position with the legs crossed (you can sit on a pillow or blankets for added comfort).

- Inhale through the nose for the count of six and breathe to fill up the entire body.

- Exhale through the nose to the count of four.

- Repeat 5-10 times or as many times as needed.

- Exercise: Inhale and sweep the arms out to the side and up overhead, lifting tall from the sides. Join the palms together and on your exhale, pull them straight down to your heart in a prayer position. Imagine the breath as lifting you taller as you reach up and as you pull the hands to your heart, come to center.

Tip: Energizing breath should emphasize the inhalations so as to pull in as much oxygen as you can to your brain, blood system, and nervous system. Lifting the arms up on your inhales helps to open the lungs and stimulate deeper breathing. This should aid in energizing the entire body.

- **Find a way to laugh**: Whether you've recently found out you miscarried, have to use donor eggs, or you just had a failed donor cycle, the last thing you may feel like doing is laughing. However, life is going to continue to offer you a series of challenges even after you have your much longed for baby. Several studies have been performed supporting the benefits of "humor therapy." Some of the best advice we can offer is to remember to find reasons to enjoy the journey. Many times at funerals or memorial services, you'll find people retelling funny stories about their lost loved ones as a way of not only remembering but releasing the grief. When we experience tragedies in general, whether caused by Mother Nature, the realities of war, poverty, or other adverse circumstances, we find a way to make up jokes that help us deal with the intensity of the sadness. This continues to be true in your own life as you experience the heartaches that happen along the road to building your family. Just a few things that laughter can do are as follows:

- Reduce stress

- Trigger endorphins

- Release pent-up negative energy

- Increase memory and learning abilities

- Increase blood and oxygen flow

- Help fight disease

And perhaps an end-of-chapter joke will help you to laugh through, what is for anyone (regardless of circumstance) an emotionally charged journey:

Q: "How many infertility patients does it take to screw in a light bulb?"

A: "Screw in a light bulb . . . hmm. Do you think that might help me get pregnant?"

9

Leaving the Nest: Recipient Parents, Donors, and Honest Questions

There's no arguing that the road you've traveled thus far hasn't been easy; and if you'd had the choice, you certainly wouldn't have signed up for this! From countless doctor's visits to the seemingly endless stacks of paperwork and legalese, no one ever thought that building a family would have so many moving parts. However, the journey you're on will offer so many new ways to appreciate and look at this new life you will have a hand in creating. In this chapter, we'll discuss some of the issues that intended parents face, especially emotional ones, as they get closer to their goals and go on to build their families.

The degree to which people mourn the loss of their genetics and move to a different approach to having a family will vary. In addition to your own acceptance, there may also be outside influences pulling you in different directions. How does your partner feel about egg donation? Have you shared this with your family? Are they supportive and open to the idea or give you static for your decisions? Never forget that there are numerous professionals who are able to help you address every aspect of your decision to pursue egg donation to build your family (not to mention the wonderful young women who are willing to share their genetic gift). And although there will be brighter days and then the more harrowing ones where you wish building a family was as simple as it seems to be for everyone else, our hope with this chapter, as it has been throughout this book, will let you know that you're not alone.

If you're confident in choosing egg donation as a means to achieve your family goals—that's fantastic! But for the rest of you, don't feel for one moment like there is something wrong about not immediately embracing this road. There are so many things to consider, and your brain is probably chock full of questions (and when you answer one, a new one pops up in its place). Don't worry—you're normal! *You* are the reason we are writing this book. We have heard the same questions, concerns, fears, and emotions from *all* of our intended parents and understand this is a process that does not see ethnicity, financial status, sexual preference, or age—it affects everyone traveling the road on some level. But the upside? This is a common bond that you share with *thousands* of other people out there and thousands more will experience this after you. Although you might not know them, there's an easy way to feel more connected with them. It is everyone else in the doctor's office waiting room. Go back to the Introduction—it's all of those people, too. They're with you in the grocery store and at church. And although they might be silent, you share a beautiful bond—one that longs for family and brings you to making decisions others could never fathom making to achieve your goal.

Throughout this book, we've leveraged the expertise of numerous reproductive industry experts to provide you with the most accurate and insightful information possible. We're continuing that tradition here with Abigail Glass who has shared with us throughout this book and who will address the most common issues that arise from start to finish with the egg donation process, arming you with some much-needed tools to help emotionally support your journey. We'll weigh in along the way with other intended parents and physicians who will share their experiences to help you along in your travels.

SHARING YOUR JOURNEY: A BRIEF DISCUSSION ON TRUST

No matter where you are in your journey, it helps to be able to confide in people you trust. It's a source of relief, and no one wants to feel like the most important people in their life don't understand why they're feeling the way they do. The bottom line is that you should share your journey with people whom you feel will be supportive, especially during your cycles, pregnancy or surrogacy, and first months after birth.

Not everyone needs to know everything right now. If you have a friend that has big opinions and you don't especially want big opinions right now, it's definitely okay to wait to share your journey with them. If you want your information to stay confidential, then tell only the people that can respect confidentiality. If you're having a tough time deciding who should know about what and when, it's an excellent time to turn to the many online support groups and message boards because you'll be interacting directly with other intended parents and parents who are having the same challenges.

FROM MY/OUR EGG TO DONOR EGG: THE TRANSITION

In Chapter 8, Wendie and Erika discussed the act of letting go. It's an incredibly powerful act for intended parents. No matter your walk of life, everyone looking at egg donation has to go through the standard stages of denial, depression, anger, blame, and acceptance regarding your genetic material. Gay intended parents never had the option to have children that are 100% genetically theirs. Lesbian intended parents would have always needed a sperm donor. Heterosexuals, whether partnered or single, probably always thought that their children would be genetically *theirs*. Egg donation, although an incredible advancement in reproductive science, has its emotional challenges, too. So how do you come to terms with making the transition from donor egg to *your* baby?

What I have seen over the years in my office is a flow of all of these feelings plus more. When someone has come to look at the possibility of donor eggs, there has generally been a difficult path of fertility treatment and disappointments. Most intended parents start with some iteration of "I want my child to be connected to me" and that makes egg donation seem like a very alternative process. Through the counseling process, I see intended parents make the shift (some more gradually than others), and egg donation becomes less of an alternative therapy and more of a viable solution. In the previous chapter, we discussed how humor could be a coping tool. There's a certain aspect of humor that comes through as well when you realize you have all of these options available through egg donors. Suddenly, you find yourself looking at photos and personalities and thinking about who you want your child to be. It becomes surreal that you begin thinking about certain aspects of your donor because most parents aren't able to get to choose things like education, looks, and athletic ability. This is the time when I start to see people laughing—and it's fabulous. *Hey, maybe it is not bad to mix in some new DNA!* or *She is beautiful! Maybe our baby will have her nose instead of mine!* It's a brilliant thing to see intended parents realize the joys in examining things that for other people are never an option.

The truth is that there is an unspoken thinking or false understanding that if we have a biological child from the sperm and egg that we "know," a child from those will be a known quantity. This simply isn't true. No parent ever knows how his or her child will turn out, whether biological, the result of egg donation, or adopted. The joy comes from embracing the process with your goals in mind and knowing that becoming a parent is more than simply genetics—it's also everything you bring to the table that will influence your child to become his or her own person.

Something I also hear quite a bit about with intended parents is how egg donation always seemed like a foreign process. Many intended parents have accepted that their situation requires the help of someone else's genetics to achieve their goal. They start going through donors, seeing what they think is important; yet throughout the entire process, it feels "weird." No matter how many donors they might consider with similar looks, education, family backgrounds, or otherwise, they just never feel at home with the process.

It's about instinct. Often a decision you make may seem or feel like the right one. Others just stink from every angle. For any intended parent, I say go with your gut, as there isn't a single intended parent I've spoken with over the years who achieved pregnancy and gave birth who ever said that her child didn't feel "hers." The goodness of the decision awaiting ahead is profoundly apparent, and that's what I try to remind couples of as they go through this process.

WILL THIS CHILD FEEL LIKE MY OWN?

When intended parents travel the path of egg donation, there's an inevitable question: Will this child feel as if it is *truly* mine? Women who conceive naturally rarely find themselves questioning the fact that their child belongs to them. But it's another question for those using egg donors because they know part of this child, at least on a genetic level, *isn't* theirs. From a professional standpoint, I'll say that parenting is more than genetics. It's environmental and behavioral because we are all creatures of habit and influence. Perhaps a path to acceptance for some parents will be seeing their child as a part of the greater universe and that although some influence will come from you and your parenting, other influences will come from your child's natural discovery process that is completely independent of you. This is the same way you and I both developed, with influence from those who surrounded us as well as lessons learned from our own curiosities. One of Wendie's intended moms, who has children from her own eggs as well as donor eggs has her own story to share as a mother on this point.

Once I found out that we were pregnant with twins, so many thoughts swirled around my head. One that I remember vividly was, "Will I be able to love these babies as much as my daughter whom I had naturally? Will they feel like mine?" During the process, I knew in my head that the eggs were not mine, but once they had been transplanted and I became pregnant, they were no longer a donor's eggs. They were tiny embryos that would grow into the babies I would eventually deliver and grow to love. As the pregnancy progressed and I saw the babies on the ultrasound, I no longer looked at them as "the babies." They became "our babies" with names that we picked out for them. When our beautiful children finally arrived, another journey had begun. Now that my sons are almost 4-years-old, I find that there hasn't been a single moment when I noticed a difference between the two experiences. Somewhere along the way, it all just melded together.

There's also the story of a highly spirited recipient mother that Wendie was working with who was so nervous about choosing a donor and coming to terms with her choice that Wendie wasn't completely sure she would ever take this step. Luckily, she made a donor selection, is now a mother, and recently wrote her an e-mail expressing her thoughts on her being connected with her baby boy.

> How do I feel now after getting to know my amazing angel of a donor who gave me the greatest gift on earth, and now that I can wrap my arms around my scrumptious sweetie pie of a boy who smiles at his mama with a big grin and two dimples to boot? I am on top of the world. I am having a profound parenting experience. Am I connected to him? If I were anymore connected to him, my partner and dog would have to move out of the house as our love affair is just over the top! His face just lights up when I am near as mine does when I'm near him. We are in love with one another *big time.*

BIOLOGICAL CONNECTIONS: QUESTIONS FOR PARTNERS (ABIGAIL GLASS, MFT, AND WENDIE WILSON-MILLER)

If you're part of a couple on an egg donation path, you'll be faced with more questions than those who are pursuing single parenthood. There may come a discussion between gay couples and heterosexual couples alike whether to use both donor eggs and donor sperm, so the baby doesn't feel like it's more one partner's than the other's. For lesbian couples, the question also arises if one partner doesn't have viable eggs, should they opt for donor eggs in that case to avoid feeling as if one couple has a genetic "advantage"? These are deeply personal decisions and ones best explored prior to your cycle, and ones that prove to be more difficult for some couples than for others.

Prior to finding out that you needed an egg donor, it's possible that you spoke with your partner about the things you hoped your child would inherit through your shared genetics. Maybe you like your partner's eyes or would love for your child to be a talented artist just like your partner. Something to consider is that the things you love about your partner won't change if you decide to use donor eggs. It's one of the beauties of the egg donation process (and sperm donation as well). When you're looking for replacement genetics, donor profiles can offer you insight into things like personality, artistic ability, eye shape, and more. For couples that feel the need (or are faced with the need) to replace genetics for both partners, it's important to understand that the options for donors available to you give you the best possible chance for creating a child who is as close to "you" as you can get.

BUT WILL MY CHILD LOOK LIKE ME/US? (WENDIE WILSON-MILLER)

It's only natural for parents to want to gaze at their child and see parts of them reflected in their appearance. When you choose egg donation, there might be some initial doubt whether your child(ren) will look like you, in spite of all of the care you've taken to choose a donor with similar aesthetics.

One of the things that fertility industry professionals hear all the time from our parents is how often people tell them their child looks *just like them*. This has even been the case when intended mothers choose donors who don't really look a thing like them! It goes to show that environment is a major influence on how parents and their children are perceived as being similar. Expressions and mannerisms alone can make people look similar (just think about people who do celebrity impressions!). So I'd say to you that if you're worried about your child not looking exactly like you, it's something to move pretty far down your list. There are so many things that go into parent and child "looking" alike that you'll have a lifetime to see those things develop. And when they do, you'll know it when an unexpected smile takes over your face as you stare in wonder at *your* child.

SHARING YOUR JOURNEY: TO TELL OR NOT TO TELL YOUR CHILDREN? (ABIGAIL GLASS, MFT)

The moment people consider using an egg donor, they are also considering whom they should or shouldn't tell about their choice. There are many pieces to consider at this early stage and along the road once you have your child via egg donation.

As you begin to explore egg donation, consider the people in your life that you'd feel comfortable knowing about your decision. This comfort level will vary from person to person, and there is no right or wrong answer. At the same time, you should be considering your potential child. My experience in this industry has shown that the best source for children to receive information about how they were brought into this world is their parent(s). With few exceptions, I have found and believe that a child who knows his or her story and all of the age-appropriate details grows to become solid in his or her identity. When a child grows up believing something inaccurate and then discovers the truth at a later age, it can bring up a whole host of other issues in that child's development—from identity confusion to trust issues. It's a huge service to your child to provide him or her with honest answers that are appropriate for his or her age and then share his or her story more and more as he or she becomes older and is able to better understand the love required and lengths to which you went through to bring him or her into this world.

A Parent's Plan on Sharing Details With Her Children on Their Origins

[My children] are only 3 now, so we are reading stories provided by PVED to help me explain it to them in an age-appropriate way. I saw a therapist who specializes in fertility to help me carve out my lifelong plan. It's imperative that children know the truth about their origin. This information shapes their identity, which ideally leads to a well-rounded happy adult.

Oftentimes, parents delay telling their children out of fear of losing a connection with their child or not feeling like they know how to handle the conversation that will inevitably occur. My best recommendation for you is that if you find yourself facing these concerns, reach out to a therapist who specializes in reproductive and family issues. There are many therapists who specialize in the ART industry who know how to help you share with your child(ren) their story and offer you tools for the questions and concerns that might arise.

And here's something that might offer you some comfort: No parent ever wants his or her child to feel different or excluded. That's a feeling shared by parents of children naturally conceived, with a little help from medical science or those who have built their families through adoption. Every child, no matter how he or she has come to this world, will have his or her particulars (just like you and me!). It's our job as parents to help our children work through the challenges they face throughout life. Whatever "it" might be with your child, you know you're going to be dedicated to helping him or her meet that need. Embrace your future role as a parent and everything that comes along with it, and I'm confident that you'll find that sharing your child's "technical" origins with him or her will be one of the least challenging hurdles facing you. And there's no shame in asking for help. When your child learns to swim and you're not a trained swim teacher, you pay for swimming lessons. When your child wants to take dance classes, you take them to a dance school. When your child needs a coach or a teacher or tutor, you go and get one! When you need help with words or relationships, you go get a therapist or someone who specializes in helping you work through those obstacles.

Insights from a Single Father Through Egg Donation

I don't subscribe to the idea that children become scarred by things like divorce or the knowledge that they were conceived through assisted reproductive technology. They may feel different or have questions temporarily. But in my opinion, we sometimes tend to overly dramatize the effect of such problems or issues. Kids are more resilient than we give them credit for. They can handle it. In fact, it stands to reason that such things make them emotionally stronger.

I think we can all agree that we'll do whatever is in the best interest of the child, and if prevarication benefits the child, most parents will do it. Of course eventually the lie will be uncovered and, at the very least, there's going to be some drama and perhaps some tears.

Here are my thoughts on that issue and maybe other parents can find something that helps them in what I'll share.

Questions Are the Answer

A child, during the course of his or her childhood, will hear adults tell him or her this and that. And, naturally, some of it will sound hokey or not ring true. How refreshing it will be when the more complicated issues in life (love, death, divorce, friendship, responsibility, etc.) are not explained with typical contrived explanations? The child, I believe, will actually be grateful that you're forcing him or her to ask himself or herself about this and develop analytical skills.

Tone of Voice

When the child, or you as the parent, brings up the issue of creation through egg donation, the child, quite naturally, might have some anxiety. Why? Well, for starters, it makes them feel different.

Which leads me to the more important point. Although the child might instinctively feel that being created differently than other kids should be a big deal, or that it's something they need to overcome, they are, in reality, going to take their cue as to how to feel from you. And in my opinion, more powerful than the words you use is your tone of voice.

You've heard the old hackneyed phrase, "It's not what you say, it's how you say it." I'm a strong believer in that. Kids early on develop a resistance to accepting at face value everything you say (that's a good thing . . . it's called "thinking for themselves"). So they, like all of us, will have more trust in your nonverbal clues. Particularly your tone of voice.

When you talk to your child about his or her origins, of course that could be a solemn issue. And if you use a solemn, serious, and otherwise "heavy" voice, the child will feel that he or she *should* be emotionally affected by the news that he or she was conceived in a test tube.

Conversely, if your voice says, in effect, "It's no big deal," then the child will pick up on this. It makes you feel good to hear someone talk to you in that manner.

AGE-APPROPRIATE CONVERSATIONS

So, when do we begin having these conversations with our children? My recommendation is that you make them a part of your family language from early on. For some, it might be the adding of children's books into your household about the many various family types. For others, it might be the words you choose. Whatever tools you find work best for your family, they need to be age appropriate. Most children begin to ask about their birth story at a very young age. There are conversations and questions sparked by seeing their friends' parents pregnant or by people you come across in your everyday routine. This happens for all children, regardless of their story. Curiosity is one of the beauties of child development, and not only do they see things in a very different way than we do as adults, but they also challenge us to see things differently (and often).

If your child(ren) start to ask about their birth around their three-year mark, listen to their questions. See exactly the type of response they are looking for, as you'll have been waiting for this question to crop up for quite some time! It is so easy to gush with information, saying far more than is needed at that time. Simply answer what they are asking. "Was I in your tummy?" Yes. "Did you and Daddy make me?" Take a deep breath. "Yes, Daddy and I worked very hard with the help of another lady and a doctor to make the exact person that you are." If your answer is enough for them, they'll accept it and move on. If they want to hear more, they'll keep asking questions. The only time you want to give them more information than they are asking or ready for is if the reason they're asking the questions is because of something someone else said. In these cases, you'll want to feel in control of the information they receive and have its delivery be on *your* terms. Although situations like these aren't optimal, they happen. My advice is for parents to embrace them, smile, share with their children the age-appropriate truth, and help them understand the details to avoid potential confusion with other children or adults who want to have this conversation with them.

Karen's Story of Sharing

We are definitely going to tell our son that he was the product of egg dona-tion. I would never *not* tell him. Why? Well, I spoke to an attorney during this process that had her kids through both egg and sperm donation and she said something very poignant. She said, "Karen, you have to tell your kid. Once they are born, this is not about you anymore," and that just clicked and immediately the decision was made for me (my partner always wanted to tell). The moment

131

that our son came out—his life and his story began, and we as his parents were part of that. How can I be his parent, the person he is supposed to trust the most in the world and not tell him the truth? When he gets his first physical and they ask for family medical history, how can I not let him know that half of his DNA is from a wonderful donor?

For us, the big question is *when* to tell him, and I used to think the answer was as young as possible; but I don't know anymore. We are going to wait and see what type of boy he is turning out to be, his temperament, and if we feel it is too much for him to tell him super young [toddler]; we will wait until he is a little older. Right now he is so happy, I really think we will be able to tell him while he's still relatively young. We also want to think about it in conjunction with his future sibling so that in telling him, we don't tell his future sibling too young. It will be a timing issue for the both of them. We will consult a counselor versed in ART before we talk to him.

ON SPIRITUALITY, SCIENCE, AND THE POWERS THAT BE (ABIGAIL GLASS, MFT, AND WENDIE WILSON-MILLER)

Regardless of your level of spirituality, there might come a time when you question whether the universe or a higher power *wants* you to have a family, especially if your road has been ripe with challenges. It's also not uncommon for intended parents with strong spiritual backgrounds to question whether the technologies that can make their dreams more accessible are "right" and if they should be using them. In cases like these, I can offer that—whatever higher power you believe in—has also given you the resources to learn about the available options for making your dreams of family come true. Spirituality will guide those who follow these paths, and you will ultimately be the one who reconciles the desires and influences you feel from forces stronger and bigger than yourself. For some, there will also be those with stringent beliefs that feel the need to criticize others for seeking help from medical technology to build their family. Although we discussed the naysayers in Chapter 2, we'll go into a bit more detail here.

When and if you choose this path, you will inevitably be up against a certain amount of criticism because there are certain populations that either don't understand or *want* to understand the science behind your decisions. It's also possible that they don't have any previous experience of their own that can be applied empathetically to your situation. There are also those people who will automatically revert to the feeling that technology undermines the natural order of things, and therefore discount or discredit your decision to seek assistance to reach your family goals.

How you choose to handle these conversations, should they even arise, will be up to you and possibly something for you to discuss with your therapist as you make your journey. They are also issues that can arise long after you've welcomed your child into the world. What we can do is share our experience that parents who achieve their family goals via egg donation are exceedingly happy about their choice, and we have no doubt that you'll find the strength to make the best possible decision and feel confident with your path, as with any important decision you'll make in life.

YOUR RELATIONSHIP WITH YOUR EGG DONOR

Although this book is written by two former egg donors who each stay in touch with at least one of their recipients, we can tell you that there's an incredible gift for the right donor and right recipient to continue a relationship on some level. However, the answer is different for every intended parent and the right answer for you might even change over time.

You don't need to decide all of this up front, so you take at least that pressure off yourself! Many donor agencies will be happy to pass on information to your donor (with your approval, of course) about pregnancies, births, and any pictures you might care to send along. Some parents send letters to their donors or update them every year with a family newsletter (see Appendix G for a few inspiring sample letters). Whatever you decide is your comfort level, know that it's your prerogative to change your involvement at any time. You may decide to initially have contact through the retrieval, and then see how you feel. You can continue to have contact through the pregnancy, and then see how you feel. There's nothing that's unchangeable, so long as your donor is willing! I think this story from Wendie's experience offers anyone reading this book tremendous insight on how your relationship with your donor can change over time, and for the better.

> I had a donor who was approached to donate through a "friend of a friend." She met her family prior to the egg donor cycle; they took her to and from her retrieval and gave her constant updates throughout the pregnancy. The family had beautiful twins, and the donor was one of the first people to get the chance to meet them. For the next two years, the family kept in touch with the donor and even paid for her to visit them on occasion. After the third year, the mom wrote a beautiful letter to the donor explaining that words could not express her gratitude for everything she had done for them, but that at this point, she felt it was better for her to distance herself so that she can see the children as "her family" and not compare every little thing to their donor. The donor completely understood, and they were able to end on a wonderful note wishing each other a lifetime of happiness.

Most people that I (Abigail) have worked with, regardless of their desire to maintain a future relationship with their donor, keep photographs and a good deal of information from their donor's profile with them, both as a memory and in case a medical issue arises where they would need the agency to contact the donor. No matter what your desire for future contact might be and when it might change, it's a sure bet that you'll remain forever grateful for this young woman's selfless contribution that's changed your life forever.

AS THEY GROW: FEELINGS FROM ADULTS BORN VIA EGG DONATION

Given how entirely new this industry is, it's not often that professionals have the opportunity to speak with an adult who was born via egg donation. We'll see more and more in the years coming, but I can share my experiences in my career thus far. I have had adults, born from donor egg, say, "I always felt different." This is often a factor, I feel, of parents not having addressed with their child their origins and how they came into this world. It's one of the reasons that our profession advocates keeping the relationship with your children open, inviting, and honest about how they came to join you in this world. Although the decision on how to communicate with your child (and whether to communicate it at all) is ultimately yours, I can share that open and honest communication will open the doors for a lifelong dialogue with your child on not only this issue, but also others that will come up over their lifetime. I'll share a story from Wendie that makes this point beautifully.

> Wendie attended a convention put on by reproductive industry professionals and sat in on a panel composed of children born from donor eggs. The panel included several children ranging from ages 3 to 15 years. The moderator asked the oldest boy, approximately 14, if he felt any different as a result of his mom having used an egg donor to bring him into the world. "Other than my superpowers," he said, "I don't notice any differences."

Another reason an adult child might feel different is if their parent(s) hadn't come to terms completely with their decision to use donor eggs to build their family. Children become a product of their environment, and it's unlikely you want to raise your child in a world filled with your doubt. My advice is to work through any issues you might have regarding egg donation *before* you disclose it to your child so that your child will receive and accept the "specialness" of who they are rather than taking on any residual issues that might exist from you not having completely come to terms with your decision. This process for you might span from your egg donor cycle all the way into a few years following your child's birth. The most important thing to keep in mind is that you're doing this to allow not only yourself to move on with your life without these burdens, but also for your child to grow up in a loving world where his or her parent(s) has no doubt whatsoever that they made the best decision and are grateful for the outcome.

10

Everyone Builds a Different Kind of Nest: Gay, Lesbian, Transgendered, Single, and International Recipients Seeking Treatment in the United States

Guest authored by
Elliott Kronenfeld, LICSW, Guy Ringler, MD,
Kathryn Kaycoff-Manos, MA,
and Lauri de Brito,
with contributions by
Wendie Wilson-Miller and
Erika Napoletano

From the very beginning, we knew that we wanted to include a much-ignored segment of the egg donation field: alternative and international families. With all of the information available in print on the subject of egg donation, our industry was definitely due for a tune-up to address these two emerging populations. Throughout Wendie's career, she's seen a steady increase in both types of recipient parents, and this chapter is dedicated to answering questions and ensuring that your journey is as obstacle free as possible.

If you're from outside of the United States and considering traveling to the United States for your egg donation procedure, you're not alone. We'll explore considerations for international recipients so you can be prepared for the options available as well as the differences in the U.S. egg donation system and that of your home country. The egg donation culture in the United States is significantly different than those in other nations and offers parents numerous options beyond what they currently have available at home. We look forward to explaining your options so you can make the best possible decisions for you and your reproductive needs.

A BIT ON "ALTERNATIVE" FAMILIES

Because we believe that the feeling of family is universal, we don't truly consider any type of family to be "alternative." However, the world is an entirely different place than it was 50 years ago, and that means there are new populations coming forth and openly expressing their desire to have children. The most important thing to remember is that all individuals and families pursuing egg donation come to this path for the same reason: They need an extra helping hand from medical technology to achieve their dreams. You're no different—and we're here to provide you with expert insights from Guy Ringler, MD, one of the reproductive endocrinologists at California Fertility Partners; Elliott Kronenfeld, community development manager at Circle Surrogacy; and Kathryn Kaycoff-Manos and Lauri de Brito with Agency for Surrogacy Solutions Inc. and Global IVF. These professionals' respective practices are making incredible inroads in working with alternative families, and we hope you'll find them to be powerful resources for your family building needs.

But now, we'll let the experts share their insights with you and we'll be seeing you throughout this chapter with our insights as well!

A BRIEF HISTORY OF ALTERNATIVE FAMILIES AND EGG DONATION (ELLIOTT KRONENFELD, LICSW)

Now, more than ever, children are being born into families headed by LGBT (lesbian, gay, bisexual, transgendered) parents. It is a new and interesting world for these families that have had their start in egg donation and/or surrogacy. Musicians, actors, and public figures having babies with the assistance of egg donation/surrogacy, as well as movie and television story lines, have brought these wonderful options to the forefront—just think of Melissa Etheridge and Elton John, to name a few. Around the world, intended parents are flocking to the United States for egg donation and surrogacy assistance because of the legal protections and advanced medical protocols as well as our culture's social acceptance of assisted reproduction.

We're living in an era that can be referred to as the Gayby Boom. It's come about for many reasons, but the most prevalent could be a greater acceptance of openly gay and lesbian individuals and couples in communities throughout the United States. Their desire to parent and build families is no different than any heterosexual couple, so let's have a look at how the LGBT communities have paved the way for modern-day egg donation and surrogacy practices.

In the earlier years of the Gayby Boom when gay parents started having children that were not from a previous heterosexual union, women led the way. Through sperm donation and insemination, lesbian moms began to create families that were as stable and successful as their heterosexual counterparts. Most lesbian couples are able to create their families through simple insemination rather than full IVF. As gay men began entering the Gayby Boom, the options weren't so easy. Socially, people understood women having children as "single mothers" but couldn't understand single or partnered men raising children. Even in the most liberal of communities, gay men were faced with social ignorance about their ability to successfully parent without a woman in the house. Men have traditionally been socialized to "leave the child rearing to the women." As one openly gay man recalled, "Every time I told someone I was going to have a child, they would ask me who was going to raise it." With those types of questions, it is no wonder LGBT intended parents have been so focused on every step of the process. Luckily, in the past two decades men have been taking more of an emotional leadership role in families that has helped redefine the role of fatherhood.

FAMILY BUILDING FOR GAY MEN (ELLIOTT KRONENFELD, LICSW, AND GUY RINGLER, MD)

Gay men who would like to have their own biological children have two options available: traditional or gestational surrogacy. These two forms of surrogacy are distinguished by who provides the eggs. In traditional surrogacy, the surrogate ovulates and is inseminated with sperm from the intended parent. The baby is the genetic mix of the surrogate's egg and the intended parent's sperm. In contrast with gestational surrogacy, embryos are created using the eggs of a designated donor and the intended parent's sperm. The embryos are then transferred into the gestational surrogate's uterus. The child has no genetic connection to the egg donor.

There are pros and cons to each type of surrogacy. Because traditional surrogacy is simpler and requires fewer medical procedures, the costs are much less than gestational surrogacy, thereby providing an economic advantage for patients. However, because the birth mother has a genetic link to the child, the legal issues regarding parenthood could become more complex in case any dispute should arise regarding parental rights. The laws defining parenthood vary from state to state, and it is essential to consult with a reproductive attorney when choosing the type of surrogacy to follow.

In gestational surrogacy, a separate egg donor is selected to create the embryos. The donor eggs are then fertilized with sperm from one or both of the intended parents, offering the opportunity to continue one or both of the intended parents' heritages (see sidebar by Elliott Kronenfeld). Because the child will have no genetic connection to the birth mother, it is more legally defined by prior case law and less risky should problems or disputes arise between parents and surrogate.

New Trends for Gay Couples and Egg Donation
Elliott Kronenfeld

There is a growing trend among gay couples where they will find an appropriate egg donor and split the total number of eggs that are retrieved into two dishes. Each man will then donate sperm to fertilize half the eggs. The reproductive endocrinologist (RE) will then take the best embryo from each set of embryos and transfer them to the gestational surrogate in the hopes of having biologically linked twins from both fathers. If a twin pregnancy is realized, both men get to be biological fathers at the same time. If this is a procedure that you and your partner find interesting, be sure to discuss the options with your reproductive specialists prior to committing to a path of treatment. They can also advise you on sperm viability for each partner and let you know if ICSI (see Glossary) is a recommended course of action to increase fertilization rates.

Technology Considerations for Gay Men and Egg Donation

As is the risk with heterosexual men, sperm function can be found to be at levels that aren't optimal for natural conception. For men who are found to have compromised sperm function as assessed by semen analysis, there are certainly technologies in use at reproductive clinics across the country to offer you the opportunity to conceive. Because the success of insemination depends on having an adequate amount of normal functioning sperm, those with male factor infertility ranging from sperm count, motility, or morphology can opt for IVF or ICSI to achieve viable embryos prior to implantation in a surrogate. The ICSI procedure allows fertilization rates of 70%–75% and involves the direct injection of sperm into the donor eggs under the microscope to enhance fertilization rates. The overall pregnancy rate per embryos transferred will depend largely on the age of the egg donor, approaching 75%–80% with eggs from young donors to approximately 40% for women at 40 years of age.

Increased fertilization and pregnancy rates aren't the only place where gay men stand to gain in their quest to build a family. Today, HIV-positive intended fathers can now have biological children. Through a special protocol that "washes" the sperm of HIV-positive men with no detectable viral load, a sperm sample can be frozen and used for IVF procedures that pose no risk of transmission to the gestational surrogate or the child. Reproductive science is making incredible inroads to ensuring that the widest possible spectrum of individuals can achieve their family building goals. This advance with the HIV-positive community is not only significant for the LGBT community, but the heterosexual community as well, demonstrating that yet another miracle of medical technology is looking out for those who desire to be parents.

DECIDING TO MOVE FORWARD WITH EGG DONATION AND SURROGACY (ELLIOTT KRONENFELD, LICSW, KATHRYN KAYCOFF-MANOS, MA, AND LAURI DE BRITO)

Seemingly simple questions such as *How? Who? Which process?* and *How do we protect our family?* have become standard conversations for LGBT intended parents that don't necessarily have easy answers. Making the decision to move forward with egg donation and/or gestational surrogacy is often the *easiest* decision, whether it's from a lack of genetic material required for your family or other considerations and complications faced by transgendered or lesbian women. So what happens next?

Intended parents have to decide if they are going to try to "go independent" and manage the entire process by themselves or find a reputable agency that will manage the process for them. We must advise that going independent is a process fraught with unnecessary risk. Although it can be done, having appropriately trained professionals to guide you is essential for your own protection as well as those who have agreed to join you on the journey—from your partner to your egg donor, surrogate, and other individuals. It is recommended that you interview several agencies before agreeing to work with them. Although you can always consult the resources provided by Wendie and Erika in Chapters 4, 5, and 6 for selecting a reproductive clinic, egg donor agency, and egg donor, we've created a list especially for those in the LGBT community who need to select a sensitive and experienced group of professionals for their journey.

Here are some considerations for selecting an egg donor/gestational surrogacy agency for LGBT intended parents:

- Have they worked with LGBT families in the past?
- Do they understand the legal concerns of LGBT families?
- Are their donor/surrogate applicants open to working with LGBT families, and how are those connections supported by the agency?
- How long has the agency been in existence?
- How many babies have they helped bring to waiting families?
- Are they a "matching" agency that will ensure that you get an appropriate match, or are they a "full service" agency that will assist you in managing the journey until you are home with your child?
- Do they have lawyers, social workers, medical personnel, and case managers on staff?
- How do they screen their egg donor and/or surrogacy applicants, and what background information is available to you?
- What is the waiting time to get matched with an egg donor/gestational surrogate that meets your needs?

- Have they ever had any legal cases brought against them?
- Do you like them?
- How much do they charge?

One of the reasons the United States has become a world leader in egg donation and gestational surrogacy is the clear safety of the legal system in most states. In 1993, the Supreme Court of California in *Johnson v. Calvert,* relying on the parties' surrogacy agreement, established that legal parentage can be determined by looking at the intentions of the parties and found that the intended mother was the sole legal mother of the child born. This case has helped to secure intended parent rights in the 44 states that are recommended for gestational surrogacy (see Appendix H for this list of states with favorable laws).

EVALUATING AGENCIES, FEES, AND EMOTIONAL CONSIDERATIONS FOR ALTERNATIVE FAMILIES (ELLIOTT KRONENFELD, LICSW, KATHRYN KAYCOFF-MANOS, MA, AND LAURI DE BRITO)

Fees are a big component of choosing how to move forward. The majority of fees should be for the actual cost of the journey, although the agency will need to cover its overhead expenses. Costs should come in a variety of categories:

- Agency fees
- Insurance (health, medical, accidental death, etc.)
- Donor and/or gestational surrogate stipends and expenses
- Legal fees
- Medical expenses (will vary based on what clinic you use and what services are required)
- Trust management
- Others

The costs for successfully completing an egg donation/gestational surrogacy depend on what you need to move forward. Do you need a biological donor but no gestational surrogate? Do you need a gestational surrogate with no biological donor? Do you need egg and sperm? Some broad parameters on current cost can be made. The American Society for Reproductive Medicine (ASRM), along with the Food and Drug Administration (FDA), set the medical and business parameters that all agencies and medical centers have to work within. As Wendie and Erika have mentioned in Chapter 6, the average compensation for egg donors in the United States is between $5,000 and $10,000, with some cases being slightly higher. Surrogate fees are not set in stone, but intended parents have been experiencing surrogate fees that usually start around $20,000 and go as high $40,000 or more per pregnancy.

In addition to what you need to be successful, there are other factors that can affect overall cost. If you are using a gestational surrogate, multiple pregnancy, C-section delivery, bed rest, or other factors can add to your overall cost. You should be prepared for a low end of $70,000 and a high end of $140,000 based on whether you are using an egg donor and/or a surrogate.

A Word on International Surrogacy Arrangements

A growing trend in the past few years has been the increased use of surrogates outside of the United States. Unlike in the United States where laws are dictated on a state-by-state basis, engaging in surrogacy arrangements outside of the country leave you at the mercy of another country's laws. Although there are many favorable outcomes, we'd do you a disservice if we didn't provide you with the basic pros and cons of these types of arrangements.

One of the most attractive things about securing a foreign surrogate is the considerable cost savings compared to a U.S. surrogate. Compared to the $70,000 to $140,000 ballpark listed earlier, a surrogate in India, for example, can cost only $20,000 to $60,000. But along with these costs savings go some disadvantages to a U.S.-based surrogacy arrangement:

- Loss of control, no direct monitoring of surrogate's living situation, and medical care
- Potential language barriers
- Potential legal complications for determining parental rights to your child

For example, although countries like South Africa, Georgia, Ukraine, and Armenia have favorable legislation to protect intended parents, others like Thailand offer intended parents no discernible rights once a pregnancy is achieved. India is working on improving its legislation, but those considering international surrogacy arrangements should have a thorough understanding of the legal situation in the country where their surrogate resides.

Costs Versus Goals

One of the best ways to control overall costs is to think long term. Don't think about having a pregnancy or a child. Think about what your family will look like when it is complete. Before beginning your journey to create your LGBT family, consider the following checklist to help you plan your finances and think through some of the more important issues:

- How long have you been planning on having children? Have you spent time with children of all ages?
- Are you hoping for twins? Do you know anyone that has raised twins and talked to them about their experience? Have you talked about the medical risks of a multiples pregnancy with your doctor?
- Does it matter to you if your children are biologically linked?
- If you are partnered, who will be the biological donor or will you both try to be biological parents?
- If you will not try to have twins from both biological donors, but you think that both of you will eventually want to be biological fathers, will you create all of your embryos now by splitting your donation?
- If you want to have additional children, but run out of embryos, how will you feel if your original donor is unavailable for another donation?
- How will you explain this process to your friends and family?
- How will you explain this process to your children? How will you help them understand why they have same gender parents?
- Will you choose an identifiable or anonymous donor?
- What will your relationship be with your donor and/or surrogate before, during, and after the pregnancy?
- What are your thoughts about your children's requests to meet their donor and/or surrogate?
- What are your views on termination and selective reduction?

Answering these questions and reviewing these topics with a knowledgeable agency should put you on track for a successful egg donation/surrogacy. Although new questions will come along as you make your journey, just remember the end goal and nothing will seem to be too overwhelming for you and/or your partner.

THE SURROGACY PROCESS (GUY RINGLER, MD)

The path to parenthood often begins with a consultation with a surrogacy agency. The role of your surrogacy agency is to conduct initial recruitment and screening of surrogate candidates; match prospective parents with surrogate candidates; organize referrals to reproductive attorneys, clinical psychologists, and reproductive endocrinologists; and to oversee the process from start to finish. As Elliott mentioned, there are both "matching" agencies and "full-service" agencies. During your interview process, you can determine how much service your agency will provide and how much you would like to receive.

The surrogacy contract establishes the intended parent's intent to have a child and thereby define parental rights. Because the laws governing parental rights vary from state to state, it is imperative to use an attorney familiar with the laws in the state where the surrogate resides and intends to give birth. As Elliott mentioned in the previous section, there is case law precedent that protects the parental rights of intended parents, so there is no need to worry that your surrogate will have any claim to the child you create.

Intended parents should also make sure that they explore the state in which they intend the birth to take place. This is a leading factor in ensuring that the legal contracts you have drawn up protect your rights as intended parents. For example, Texas (as of the publication of this book) only recognizes surrogacy contracts for legally married heterosexual couples. In cases such as this, there would be more favorable states in which to arrange for birth of your future child via surrogate, and you should discuss these details with both your surrogacy agency and reproductive law attorney.

The surrogacy agency reviews candidates' applications, obtains past medical records, conducts background checks, arranges psychological assessments of candidates, and confirms insurance coverage before presenting candidates to prospective parents. The medical screening may or may not be carried out prior to a match meeting between intended parent and surrogate.

It is important for the surrogacy agency to match the expectations of the surrogate mother with those of the intended parents for the pregnancy experience. Some intended parents want to become very involved with their surrogate throughout the pregnancy whereas others prefer a more distant relationship. Naturally, this is something that goes both ways with surrogates as well. Provided that both sides meet the expectations, the experience should be positive and supportive throughout the pregnancy. Given that the surrogacy process is one steeped in emotions from all parties, it is important to meet the needs and expectations of both parties and have clear understandings up front. And don't be afraid to ask for referrals from previous clients. You're about to enter into a relationship that could last up to a year, so getting insights from parents who have used your agency of choice before entering into an agreement could help you avoid a costly mistake or reinforce the gut instinct you have to proceed.

On Trust Accounts for Surrogacy

The surrogacy agency or the attorney will usually establish a trust account to provide payment to the surrogate at appropriate points during the process. When you hear about surrogacy firms making headlines (and in all the wrong ways), it usually has something to do with misappropriation of funds. Bottom line? Never work with a surrogacy agency that holds your funds. Only an attorney or a bonded escrow company should hold your funds.

Understanding Your Surrogate

Once a match is made, your chosen surrogate will undergo a complete medical screening. The goal of surrogacy screening is to attempt to provide a healthy environment for the developing fetus. A complete physical exam including a pelvic exam, Pap smear, pelvic ultrasound, and uterine evaluation is performed. Blood and urine tests for infectious diseases (potential surrogate and sexual partner/spouse) and urine drug screens are conducted. Without exception, surrogates must have had at least one normal, uncomplicated pregnancy with delivery. Her past medical and pregnancy histories should be free of any factors that might put future pregnancies at risk. The goal of surrogacy screening is to provide as best as possible a healthy environment for the developing fetus, and these medical examinations and review of the surrogate's pregnancy history are the most effective ways to ensure that she can uphold her commitment to help you grow your family.

As you select your surrogate and prepare to enter into this important relationship, there are a few things to remember to help make your journey an easier one. First, your surrogate is a person of her own, with her own life, needs, friends, and family. Although she is also someone who is opting to share her body with you to help you achieve your dreams, you'll have to be comfortable with giving up some control so she can continue to be her own person. However, you do have a say in many of the processes and your contracts should be constructed in such a way that you understand how your surrogate will be communicating and expected to act for the duration of your surrogacy.

For example, there should be a Health Insurance Portability and Accountability Act (HIPAA) release in place so that you can communicate directly with your surrogate's OB/GYN throughout the pregnancy, but you shouldn't expect (or request) a list of everything your surrogate's eaten each day for the past week. Respecting that your surrogate is her own person and committed to seeing this process through is a big leap of faith, but one you'll need to be prepared to take. You should also have the conversation up front about birthing expectations and your presence at the delivery. Every OB/GYN has different guidelines about who and how many people can be present in a birthing room, so working out details like these ahead of time can save you headaches later on and ensure you get the experience you desire.

Once you've covered all of these details with your surrogate and she's completed a successful medical and medical history screening, you'll coordinate the duration of the process with your egg donor agency and chosen donor. Use Chapter 6 in this book as a guide to help you through the egg donor selection process.

Legal Considerations for LBGT Intended Parents
(Guy Ringler, MD)

To help ensure the legal safety of your family, it is important to have several legal documents created both before and during your egg donation/surrogacy. Each intended parent should have a will finalized prior to undergoing IVF. A will should detail who would receive the rights to any unused embryos as well as who will take custody of your child if one of the intended parents should die during the surrogacy pregnancy, in addition to any other survivor's rights and transfers of property you want to ensure. Health care proxies should also be explored, as they allow partners to make health care decisions for each other should one partner become incapacitated. Powers of attorney allow partners to make decisions for each other. This becomes even more important in situations where LGBT partners can't be legally married. Although these laws are changing quickly across the country, a power of attorney will help most same-sex couples act in the best interests of the other should one become incapacitated.

When a child is born in the United States, that child will automatically be a U.S. citizen and can be issued a U.S. passport within days of the birth. This is extremely important when intended parents live outside of U.S. borders. It will facilitate their ability to return to their home country with ease when ready to travel with a new family member. What goes on the child's birth certificate is based on what is allowed in the state where the child is born and what information is required by laws of the intended parents' home location. Making sure that you can have the information you desire and need on the birth certificate in your unique situation is important. Many states will allow for a second parent (same sex) adoption. This is one of the many reasons you should speak with an attorney knowledgeable in the laws of the state where you'll be finalizing your egg donation and surrogacy agreements.

Legal Paperwork for Your Child

Your child's legal paperwork is based on several factors: insurance coverage, the current laws available to give the intended parents legal rights, and the requirements of the intended parents' home location. Some intended parents are able to get prebirth orders that will name them as parents prior to birth, whereas others will perform a single- or second-parent adoption after the birth. For international gay intended parents, this decision is often based on what they need to be able to get home legally and safely with their new child. It is important that you speak with a surrogacy agency as well as a qualified legal professional that understands all of the legal implications of an egg donation/surrogacy journey to ensure that your family is properly protected. If you are intended parents who live outside the United States, it might be possible to complete a second-parent adoption in your home country, based on your country's laws. You should consult a legal professional in your home country to explore your options.

Cycle Coordination (Guy Ringler, MD)

After you, your egg donor, and surrogate have been medically cleared and all contracts have been signed, a treatment calendar is generated that outlines the medical treatment between egg donor and surrogate. In this process, the menstrual cycles are suppressed in both the donor and surrogate to allow for synchronization of the surrogate's uterine lining with the egg donor's stimulation cycle. After both cycles are sufficiently suppressed, estrogen is started in the surrogate to begin to prepare her uterus for pregnancy. Several days later, the egg donor begins her ovarian stimulation medication. The egg retrieval procedure can be expected to occur approximately 11–12 days later.

The intended parents may provide sperm on the day of egg retrieval, or it can be frozen at any time prior to the treatment cycle. Freezing semen samples prior to the actual cycle provides more time to obtain all required FDA results. If a fresh specimen is used in your cycle, the sperm provider must be screened within seven days of the egg retrieval, and all test results must be reviewed before the embryos can be transferred into the surrogate. For cases using fresh semen, we usually ask the intended parent to arrive five to seven days before the anticipated egg retrieval to ensure test results prior to the transfer date.

As mentioned earlier, careful attention to detail by all members of the fertility team is essential to optimizing results. The large amount of cycle preparation and coordination between all parties requires the efforts of a team, not just a few individuals. Not only are there several patients involved in a single treatment cycle, but in many cases, all individuals may not live in the same city or even the same country. Each individual/patient requires complete medical screening, informed consent, and communication during the treatment to ensure appropriate follow through of all the required lab work, checklists, and monitoring that are required during the cycle.

Your fertility clinic should have specially trained nurses and assistants to help with the careful coordination and communication between all parties and monitoring facilities. Each treatment calendar begins with planning of dates and times for all monitoring procedures and lab tests. Most of the larger IVF centers in the United States will assist in the monitoring of outside patients by ultrasound and will provide hormone testing if necessary lab orders are filed in advance and reimbursement arranged. If your egg donor is in the United States but out of state from where you'll receive treatment, a monitoring center must be identified that will provide all required testing and lab results in a timely manner. For international recipients, it is helpful to have staff members at both your surrogacy agency and fertility clinic who can speak several different languages or to have access to interpreters to ensure easy communication between facilities.

All necessary documents must be filed in advance of the test dates to ensure responsive handling, as timely transmission of lab data is necessary to allow for treatment modification and progress during the cycle. These cases are very complex and the team you help put together through your selection of egg or sperm donor, surrogate, surrogacy agency, and fertility clinic are all essential to your cycle's success.

Factors Affecting Success Rates for Surrogacy

Pregnancy rates with donor eggs and gestational surrogacy approach 80% per transfer cycle, which are the highest rates possible in reproductive medicine today. These success rates are due to the young age of the egg donors (usually between 20 and 30 years of age) and the proven reproductive track record of the gestational carriers. Other factors responsible for the high pregnancy rates include

- the careful screening of egg donors for documentation of normal ovulation cycles and normal ovarian reserve
- thorough screening of gestational carriers for excellent reproductive function including normal uterine evaluations
- careful monitoring of the ovaries during stimulation with titration of medication during the cycle and optimal timing of egg retrieval
- optimal culture conditions to ensure good embryo development
- an experienced embryology staff skilled in aspects of embryo culture, manipulation, and freezing
- reproductive endocrinologists skilled in ultrasound-guided embryo transfer techniques

We all hope for the happy day when we can call our intended parents with the news of a positive pregnancy test, only to be topped by the best day of all: when their newborn child is placed into their arms for the very first time. If you keep in mind all of the moving parts that are necessary for your egg donor/surrogacy cycle to be a success, you'll be better prepared for your emotional yet highly rewarding journey to parenthood.

FAMILY BUILDING OPTIONS FOR LESBIAN WOMEN
(GUY RINGLER, MD)

The treatment options for lesbian women are more varied than those for gay men, simply based on the fact that women come equipped to carry children and produce eggs. We understand, however, that lesbian women are subject to the same limitations and challenges as any other population of women. We'll cover the more traditional roads to family for lesbian women as well as those involving egg donation.

For a woman who desires conception using her own eggs and donated sperm, the process may be as simple as a natural cycle intrauterine insemination or IUI. In this procedure, washed donor sperm is placed into the upper uterine cavity by a narrow catheter at the time of ovulation. This treatment option requires that a woman has regular ovulation cycles and has normal patent fallopian tubes. The pregnancy rates per insemination cycle depend primarily on the woman's age with pregnancy rates of 10%–15% during the 20s and 30s, and approximately 5% after age 40. Most pregnancies will occur in the first six treatment cycles. If a pregnancy does not occur within this interval, then women will want to consider additional testing of the pelvis such as a laparoscopy and ultimately moving to IVF for higher success rates.

The pregnancy rates with IVF are several folds higher than with IUI at every age up to the mid-40s when the pregnancy rates with each treatment become similar.

For lesbian couples, there is an option of transferring embryos created by the eggs of one woman and donor sperm into the partner's uterus. This treatment requires IVF for the egg donor with embryo transfer into her partner's uterus and involves the synchronization of both women's menstrual cycles and simultaneous preparation of the partner's uterus who intends to carry the child. This treatment allows each woman to play a vital role in the conception of the child, as one woman provides the egg and the other partner gestates the child until delivery.

Consultation with a reproductive attorney is recommended to discuss parental rights for each partner. The laws defining parenthood can vary from state to state, just as in marriage, so it is essential to consult with an attorney before creating your family through assisted reproduction. You can review the earlier section contributed by Elliott Kronenfeld regarding legal considerations as an excellent start to making sure your legal needs are met prior to and after the arrival of your child.

NEW PARENTS (GUY RINGLER, MD)

After all of the planning, preparation, procedures, and payments, lives change dramatically with the arrival of a newborn child. The support of family and friends can help make the initial transition more bearable during sleepless nights. As your child grows and you become a family, you may want to seek out one of the support groups that have been built in most large American cities. In Los Angeles, there is a wonderful organization called the Pop Luck Club (www.popluckclub.org) that was created by several gay dads who met each Sunday at a park in the city to share parenting tips and adjustment tips for life as fathers. Over the years, the group has grown to several thousand members who now host monthly meetings, educational fairs, and group outings to encourage a sense of community and provide support to gay dads throughout the Los Angeles area. California Fertility Partners has supported this group for years, and we admire their strength and contribution to gay family life in the city.

Another wonderful resource is the Family Equality Council (www .familyequality.org). This group works at all levels of government to advance social and legal equality on behalf of the approximately one million lesbian, gay, bisexual, and transgender families raising more than two million children throughout the United States.

CONSIDERATIONS FOR INTERNATIONAL INTENDED PARENTS (KATHRYN KAYCOFF-MANOS, MA)

The experience of finding an egg donor in the United States can be very daunting, especially if you're coming from abroad where options are limited or not at all available. In the United States, the choices are seemingly endless, and the information on donors is quite a bit more robust in most cases. You also have a choice in the type of relationship you would like to have with your donor in many cases, from meeting prior to the donation cycle to maintaining an ongoing relationship afterward.

The one other thing that differs in the United States from other countries is the number of eggs the doctors generally seek to retrieve during a donor cycle. In other countries, the goal is 6–8 good eggs, although in the United States it is generally 12–18 eggs. Something else to keep in mind is that embryo transfers in the United States for fresh donor cycles usually call for the transfer of one or two embryos. In frozen cycles, they may transfer three or four. You can always speak with your chosen reproductive specialist on their thoughts about how to hone these numbers even further.

Although there are so many more options here in the United States, you will find that these options bring about many more questions. But along with those questions comes a beautiful array of options to help shape your family.

On International Surrogacy Arrangements: Seeking a U.S.-Based Surrogate

The sections in the chapter that address surrogacy offer comprehensive information and resources that apply to all intended parents, whether they live in the United States or abroad. However, all international recipients should be well versed on postbirth insurance.

In the United States, a newborn child is covered by the health insurance of the parents. However, as an international intended parent, you cannot use your own insurance to cover your newborn child. Surrogacy contracts will state that once the umbilical cord is cut, your surrogate is no longer responsible for the child. That means she can't use her insurance for the child either. That's where the health insurance policy comes in. If your child has no complications, it shouldn't be expensive. But complications can arise even if everything looked great throughout the pregnancy. So, what can you do? First, if you work for a multinational company, see if they have insurance that will cover you overseas—often this will also cover a child. Your surrogacy agency should have a list of insurance resources (which is why it's a smart idea to work with an agency experienced in dealing with international intended parents). In many cases, a policy like this should be sufficient. But if you don't have access to that type of policy (and many people don't), then you'll need to purchase something for those "just in case" situations to cover you until you return to your home country. "Just in case" can mean twins (who are often born early) or other complications that would warrant a longer hospital stay. For the latter, medical bills can add up quickly, and it's best to make sure you have the health coverage you and your future child or children need to return home in a healthy state without undue financial burden. Again, your agency can help you navigate the available policies and coverage limits, but it is important to remember that the insurance landscape is ever-changing. Review the policy coverage options prior to signing and then prior to birth as well.

Returning to Your Home Country with Your Child(ren)

Following birth and the assurance from your physician that all is well and you're cleared to travel, you'll need to prepare a few things to make your journey home as smooth as possible. First, you'll need the birth certificate(s) and, in most cases, you'll request that the hospital expedite the process of getting those to you.

Second, you'll need to obtain a U.S. passport for your child, as he/she will be an American citizen. You can also request these in an expedited manner (your surrogacy agency can also direct you to these resources). Once you have the passport, you can then obtain airline tickets in the name of your child(ren).

When going back to your home country, you should be aware of the laws that will govern you and your new child. If you are hoping to get a passport and citizenship in your home country and you are a woman or heterosexual couple, you may want to consider coming to the United States a month or two before the birth—that way, there won't be questions about how you could give birth to a child in the United States when you were halfway across the world.

A last bit of advice is to talk to a lawyer or a licensed legal practitioner in your home country to better understand if there are any other considerations about citizenship for your child. Knowing all of the legal guidelines that you'll have to navigate can make the transition back home as seamless as possible.

Specialty Clinics for International Intended Parents

Although there are many clinics that claim to specialize in assisting overseas patients, they aren't your only option. Any clinic with a wonderful reputation can likely assist you, although there are certain areas of the country that see a higher instance of international intended parents than others.

Southern California clinics tend to have a higher population of international recipients and oftentimes have a variety of resources available to help them in the most efficient manner possible. Some have staff members that speak a variety of languages, and others have a facilitator dedicated to working exclusively with their international clients. It's good practice when calling a clinic to ask how often they deal with international clients, and do they have someone on staff that will help manage your specific needs choose. In many cases, the agency can help you with everything from recommending hotels to travel arrangements. It simply depends on the extent to which they've built their service offerings to cater to their international clientele.

If you are working with a surrogacy or egg donor agency, they may help direct you to the clinics that have more experience with international patients. The same holds true for these agencies—ask them how many international clients they have worked with and from what countries. You want to make sure you are not a test case for helping someone from overseas.

11

The Nest of the Future

Guest authored by
Bradford Kolb, MD, and Daniel Potter, MD,
with contributions from
Wendie Wilson-Miller and Erika Napoletano

There is no doubt that advances in medical science have helped humankind tremendously over the years. Diseases that once decimated entire populations have been eradicated. The types of medicine offered in most industrialized countries are readily available and help treat and control a wide berth of ailments and conditions. Those who have struggled and continue to struggle with infertility now have options and opportunities to expand their families that previous generations could never have conceived (pun intended). Through the continued advancement in science and technology along with breakthroughs in the human genome project, the ART field will continue to discover better ways to help families get pregnant with greater efficiency. Let's have a look at what the past 60 years have brought to the field of assisted reproduction:

1954: First successful pregnancy using frozen sperm.

1968: First known embryo biopsy performed on rabbits.

1969: First successful IVF of an immature human egg (oocyte).

1978: The world's first test tube baby was born.

1983/84: First IVF baby using frozen embryos. First egg donor baby conceived.

1986: First IVF baby using sperm retrieval surgery.

1989: First unaffected child born following PGD testing for an X-linked disorder.

1992: First Microinjection Intra-Fallopian Transfer (MIFT) baby was conceived.

1997: First successful birth using frozen eggs.

2003: Sixty-five-year-old woman becomes the oldest known woman to give birth by using donated eggs and sperm.

The advantages today for those aspiring to being parents are tremendous in comparison to what reproductive science looked like back in the 1950s. For medical and other reproductive industry professionals, acknowledging this and educating patients and parents alike is key. We see changes every year, and it's our job to introduce those changes to the right parents who can benefit from them at the right time. So take heart—although there might be a challenge facing you today, tomorrow might very well be another story.

WENDIE'S TAKE ON NEW TECHNOLOGY

Back when Erika and I started in this industry—a little more than 10 years ago—success rates for egg donation were around 40%. It was also commonplace for most injections to be given via intramuscular injection with a 1½″ needle. The medications were in glass vials and required mixing. Egg donors had to break off the tops of the vials and mix all of the medications together, sometimes mixing up to six vials of sterile solution and powder at once. It almost seemed like a chemistry degree was required to make sure the medication was taken correctly!

Erika Weighs in on the History of Donor Injections

My first egg donor cycle was in 2001, and I remember well opening the box that arrived at my house, finding it filled with boxes and boxes of glass vials and giant Ziploc bags of syringes. I stared at the entire ordeal and thought, "You've got to be kidding me." At my next screening appointment, they reviewed all of the medications with me and then twice a day for nearly 11 days, I set up my own little chemistry lab in my guest bathroom. I'd line up vials of powder next to the ampoule of sterile solution and mix, mix, mix. Then I'd reach back behind me, take a deep breath and stick that 1½″ needle into my glute and feel the burn. When I heard that, today, donors get these neat little injection pens—I won't lie—I was jealous!

Today, most egg donor medications are given in a premeasured pen and taken via subcutaneous injection. Cycle success rates using are now closer to 60%–70% with donor eggs, and processes like vitrification are making frozen embryo transfers nearly as successful as fresh cycle transfers.

WHAT LIES AHEAD FOR EGG DONOR TECHNOLOGY? (BRADFORD KOLB, MD, AND DANIEL POTTER, MD)

There are things that are already waiting in the wings as well as some technologies and processes further along the horizon that will not only increase the chances of first-time transfer success, but also help the babies born through ART have an even greater chance of a healthy, disease-free life.

Here are a few things already slated for the short term in the assisted reproductive field (within five years or less):

Embryo Quality

Currently, when embryos are created through egg donation, about half or even more than half are going to be chromosomally abnormal. To have a baby, you need a chromosomally normal and metabolically competent embryo. Once you have both, the success rate increases. Right now, physicians and embryologists are just starting to use technologies to determine if an embryo is chromosomally and metabolically competent. The 24-chromosome genetic screening (a process by which all of the chromosomes in a cell are evaluated) is just starting to be used and studied.

This process involves using microchips that allow for the testing of thousands of segments of the DNA. These are called microarrays. The technology amplifies the DNA from a single cell to create enough DNA so that it can be measured. The DNA is then analyzed using microarrays to determine how many chromosomes are in the embryo. A similar technology is emerging that involves the sequencing of DNA, mainly to greater efficiency to determine genetic normality of the embryo. The hope that as these technologies continue to emerge, the embryo chosen for transfer from this process increases the chance of implantation to 90% or higher.

Laboratory Innovation and Experimentation

New additives and techniques are improving at a rapid rate. Specialists work day in and day out to refine and improve the lab environments and culture methods to increase the percentage of genetically sound and strong embryos.

157

A new and promising technology involves time-lapse photography to monitor how the cells in an embryo divide. Using this information, embryologists can better predict the most viable embryo to transfer and may allow the transfer of embryos at the Day 3 stage without requiring them to develop to the blastocyst stage.

Embryo Cultures

The conditions under which embryos are cultured are seeing rapid advancements. The mixture and gas types of incubators being used and other processes are being tested right now in labs all over the world. The outcome will hopefully result in better environments for embryos to grow, meaning a higher embryo quality and a lower attrition rate from retrieval to fertilization to implantation and potential freezing.

Genetic Carrier Conditions

The ability to accurately screen people for hundreds of genetic diseases relatively quickly or inexpensively is already making its way into most clinics. These tests can now be performed using a cotton swab on the inside of egg donors' mouths. From our perspective, these testing protocols are poised to become the industry standard within the next five years.

There are also things a bit further down the road that will be making their way into mainstream reproductive practices as well. We expect to see the advancements that follow come to the mainstream over the next 5–10 years.

Medications

Right now, it's a common understanding with egg donors that they'll be self-administering injections for approximately three weeks. In the next several years, intended parents and donors alike may also have the option of taking orally active hormonal medications instead of injections. There are also medications making their way through FDA trials that offer the potential for fewer injections throughout the course of a cycle.

Genetic Markers

As we get more information from the decoding of the human genome, there is the chance that researchers will discover certain genetic markers that could predict the response a donor and/or intended mother will have to fertility medications. This would be based on identifiable genetic factors or patterns that would lead researchers and physicians to predict how the egg donor or IVF patient will respond to a particular protocol. They might also shed light on or predict a response to fertility drugs that would allow physicians to better customize stimulation protocols for a patient's specific genetic profile.

Although it's risky to place too much importance on what the future might hold from a scientific standpoint, what we can reinforce is that there are specialists and researchers working tirelessly to help make family a more accessible goal for even more people. All things considered, patients need to keep in mind that technology is not going to replace the human side of the fertility equation, from conversations with partners to building relationships with your fertility specialists. Emerging technologies may enhance the quality of care—which is something that excites us as medical professionals dedicated to helping our patients achieve a certain end goal. But even more than technology, the relationships we build with our patients are what allow us to best serve them. And whichever medical professionals you decide to have accompany you on your journey toward family, we hope you feel the same way about the relationships you develop with them.

THE EVOLUTION OF EGG DONOR AGENCIES AND AGENCY COOPERATION (WENDIE WILSON-MILLER)

Our industry has changed—and for the better—over the past several years, offering us tools and resources to better serve intended parents. For example, vials of prefrozen vitrified eggs are already offered at some egg donor agencies and clinics. This option allows you to fertilize and use the eggs at the time that is most convenient for you. With the high percentage of freeze/dethaw success rates discussed in Chapter 5, the success rates have been extremely promising so far. The costs associated with using prefrozen eggs are considerably lower than pursing a fresh donor cycle, which makes egg donation a more financially accessible option for those with limited resources. We look forward to seeing more statistics come available for cycles that used vitrified eggs and in the meantime, it's an option you can discuss with select donor agencies and/or fertility clinics.

In the more immediate future, egg donation agencies are moving towards a less competitive rivalry with one another and instead finding better ways to work together for the benefit of intended parents. These changes in agency attitude and previous practices will move us all toward the best possible care for all of our recipient families.

Currently, some of the ways that agencies have reached out to one another is by establishing "donor share" programs. *Donor sharing* means that intended parents do not have to move to a different agency if they can't find a donor at the one they are currently with. Rather, agencies will share their donor databases with other agencies, making every participating agency's pool of donors even larger. This is incredibly important, especially if you have already established a bond with the agency you're currently working with and do not want to pick up and go elsewhere during an already trying journey.

Donor sharing can happen in a multitude of ways; however, the bottom line always remains the same—the intended parents should not have to pay more than the quoted agency fees with their home agency. Some agencies are willing to split the cost of a program fee to give their intended parents access to another agency's donors, regardless of what the program fee is (for example, if there is a discounted program fee, then that should also be applied for the benefit of the intended parents). Others are agreeing to universal fee arrangements for intended parents wanting to search outside their home agency. Regardless, agencies are becoming more willing to break away from their established, more independent ways and into arrangements that encourage cooperation—for everyone's benefit.

Steve Masler, CEO of The Donor Source, tells of the outlook for increased sharing between egg donation agencies:

> As one of the largest egg donor agencies in the US with 1,400 active donors in its data base, The Donor Source feels a special responsibility to support elevation of ethical standards of our industry. Accordingly, along with Wendie Wilson-Miller, we are participating in the development of an organization to be called Surrogacy and Egg Donation Ethics Society (SEDES), whose purposes will include development and facilitation of sharing mechanisms between agencies. The group will initially include four agency members from Southern California, but it will likely expand to include agencies outside Southern California as well as nonagency members such as attorneys, therapists, etc.

> The new organization will, as its name suggests, focus on developing, communicating, and supporting ethical approaches to the functions of an egg donation/surrogacy agency. One or more of the standards will likely involve sharing of donors between agencies. By working together to support each other and the industry as a whole, each agency will contribute to the elevation of the perception of agencies as a whole by fertility practices and the public.

Lilly Frost, director of My Donor Cycle, shares her experiences with donor sharing across agencies:

> Sharing donors between different cycle-coordination agencies can be a valuable service for clients who, like most potential recipients, are

looking for a donor with specific genetic traits matching their own. Because not all agencies have an extensive database of donors, they often will not be able to meet the needs of each new client relying on their database alone. Some agencies build their donor database to meet the needs of their target demographic, for example, Asian, African American, Jewish, and so forth. Others have diverse donor databases but lack the volume and variety necessary to service the individual needs of a growing client base. Inter-agency agreements to share donors provide a framework from which even the smallest agency can offer their clients a wide variety of genetic traits, without having to make a referral to another agency.

When I began My Donor Cycle, I had no donor database of my own. I would often receive referrals from clinics with limited, if any, available donors in their in-house database. The intended parents were looking for a donor with proven fertility and intelligence that also shared their physical attributes, ethnicity, and, sometimes, even their religion. At times, finding the desired donor was a classic needle in the haystack situation. To find that perfect donor, I would contact agencies throughout the nation and ask for access to their donor databases. Many agencies were reluctant to allow me access, fearing the risk of losing a donor to a competitor. But the benefits of lending donors to another agency far outweigh any risk of a competitor burning a bridge by trying to contract around the lending agency.

Stephanie Goldman-Levich, director of client services for Family Creations, has some additional thoughts:

Agencies work hard to recruit a diverse database of egg donors. While we hope that we can assist each of our clients in finding the donor that is the right match for them, it is not always possible. Anytime we as an agency can go the extra mile to help a client find a donor that makes them more comfortable, I think we should do so.

I would like to see more agencies work together in several ways. For one, I think we are in a position to share important information that can be useful to our clients: donor testing results, profile information—everything that can help intended parents make the best possible choice.

Secondly, most agencies work with many of the same professionals on a daily basis. We coordinate with the same clinics, attorneys, therapists, escrow companies, and more. Most experiences with these professionals are wonderful, but that is not always the case.

By sharing our experiences with these professionals, we can make sure we are providing our intended parents with the best referrals possible and also steer them clear of any service providers that are not up to par.

Nancy Block, RN, is the CEO for both The Center for Egg Options Illinois and The Donor Network Alliance. Nancy was also an obstetrics and fertility nurse at Northwestern Memorial Hospital in Chicago for 17 years. An agency owner/director working with egg donors and surrogates for 12 years, she talks about the benefits of donor sharing and why she chose to start Donor Network Alliance.

The Donor Network Alliance (DNA) is an aggregate of egg donors and gestational surrogates from multiple agencies posted on one site with one e-mail and one password for access. The site has a variety of information provided on each donor, each agency, as well as industry policies, how to contact each agency, and a mode of direct contact for the agency/donor coordinator. In the past, it could take days to contact each agency, get a response on donor availability, agency pricing, legal agreements, etc. Even though I am an expert in the field and know the shortcuts to finding a donor, a search for intended parents can take a considerable amount of time. Most busy professionals don't have the time or the privacy to do a search at work so they are left with evenings or weekends as available. DNA gives that time back to the intended parents.

In working with the agencies listed on DNA, they are intent on helping each intended parent and do their best to be responsive. When I've helped a client for DNA, I have had all very positive responses from other agencies. I have talked to many intended parents who have thanked the staff at DNA for starting and managing the site. Because we have over 6,000 egg donors and nearly 50 surrogates, we make ourselves available to our registered users through e-mail and phone. There are times when a client needs a little troubleshooting, additional help on the site, or for just answers to questions about egg donation and surrogacy in general. A nurse manages those calls along with our webmaster for Web site-related inquiries. While the process of searching for an egg donor or surrogate is foreign to many, especially those outside the United States, DNA helps demystify the process with no-cost guidance and a centralized location for intended parents to focus their efforts on.

Although we have only shared examples from a few agencies, this is by far not representative of all of those in our industry willing to donor share.

It is fast becoming the trend to work together for the good of our intended parents—a change we are delighted to see. Most of us who have been in this industry for several years have become accustomed to hearing our different clients' heartaches and disappointments. It is disappointing when these heartaches are added to stories of agencies that made the process harder than it needed to be. Donor sharing and organizations like Donor Network Alliance are doing wonders for our industry, and we look forward to seeing what the future holds that can make our industry even more accessible and friendly.

SHARING INFORMATION: BETTER COMMUNICATION FOR BETTER CYCLES

It's not uncommon for egg donors to register with multiple agencies in hopes of being matched with intended parents: Something that would benefit our industry greatly is the sharing of donor cycle information. This is something that will benefit everyone involved in the egg donation process. Here are some examples:

Stimulation history: Knowing how a donor responded to a particular protocol can help another fertility specialist design a favorable protocol when she's matched again.

Behavioral history: Sometimes donors are difficult to work with, just like anyone else we might encounter in life. If this information was available to intended parents, agencies, and doctors, we can all make better decisions.

Cycle history: Repeat donors would have their records consolidated, so everyone knew exactly how many times the donor had cycled and how she responded to the carrying stimulation and suppression protocols. This can help intended parents to make the best possible donor choice and guide physicians in helping their patients achieve their dreams.

In today's environment, we unfortunately see some agencies unwilling to share their donors' information with other agencies, even if it's for the ultimate benefit of both their donor and another agency's client. We believe, as do most agencies, IVF clinics, intended parents, therapists, and others directly involved with this process, that obtaining complete cycle information is the only ethical way to allow a donor to move forward with another cycle. We're optimistic about a shift in the industry's attitude toward the sharing of information because it's something that can only be universally beneficial. Because we're all in the same business, we're keeping our fingers crossed! Any agency should be able to pick up the phone and contact another on behalf of its clients. Ideas, requests, suggestions, openness, and honesty should be expected occurrences!

Although the press tends to sensationalize our industry with monetary labels like "a billion dollar industry," we don't know a single professional in this industry who feels that way about his or her career. The professionals we know chose this path because they had a profound experience that told them this would be their life's work, not unlike anyone else who builds a career based on their passion. What we can hope for in the future is an industry that grows from both technology and emotional standpoints and that offers intended parents from every walk of life the best possible chances to experience parenthood. To live it, encourage it, and demand it from those who surround us in our work environments each day and still hold every hand we can when extended toward us for a little help from medical technology.

Epilogue

Although we didn't initially plan on writing a formal wrap-up chapter for this book, we came to the end of Chapter 11 and realized there were few things we still wanted to share.

We're infinitely grateful to each of the professionals who took the time out of their careers to help us build this guide for you. Without their assistance, our insights for being egg donors and an agency owner wouldn't have had nearly the impact. The fertility industry and the road you've traveled are the ones that are both ever changing, and we hope that the information in the pages preceding have helped you figure out where to begin, what's the most important to you, and give you a sense that you're not alone.

It's strange for both of us to think back to our first egg donor cycles and what brought us each through the doors of our first donor agency, but we're grateful that's where life has taken us. What we hope for you—the intended parents we'll most likely never meet—is that you find your piece of serenity and, ultimately, a happiness in your life that's incomparable to anything you've ever imagined. While we hope that comes in part from your future children, we know that's not always the ending.

Keep faith, chin up, and know that you're never walking the road of fertility alone. We're both very fortunate to have found where we fit into your journey, the industry's history and its future, and we thank you for allowing us to share through a few hundred pages our experiences and best advice.

The Appendices follow, and there you'll find a host of information we referred to throughout this book. Highlight them, tear them out, photocopy them, or use sticky notes to tell your partner what you want him or her to read. This book is as useful as you want it to be, and we hope that it won't be very long until you no longer need it and can share it with someone else who does.

As we were approaching the end of the writing process for this book, we were struggling with what we could say to adequately express the feeling of togetherness happening among agencies, clinics, donors and parents, and the all-encompassing feeling of hope we all experience during the egg donor process. Out of the blue, Wendie received an e-mail from one of her agency's intended parents that summed it up perfectly—the reason we all do what we do on every level. She was kind enough to share her secret with Wendie, and with her permission, we're sharing it with you as well.

I have to admit, I am full of hope, joy, and a bit of nerves. But mostly hope!! Hearing that we can move forward makes it seem tangible now. I'll tell you a secret. For the last year, I have kept a onesie in my underwear drawer so that every morning, I can set the intention of bringing our baby into the world. For the past few months, I've been doing it more out of habit; but today, I went upstairs and just held it. It felt so real and true, just perfect. Please thank everyone at the agency, the nurses on our team, and especially our donor.

Wendie Wilson-Miller and Erika Napoletano

Appendix A—Interview Questions for Fertility Clinics

1. How long does an average egg donor cycle take from the time I choose a donor until transfer?

2. What do you need us to bring to our first appointment (e.g., test results, medical records, etc.)?

3. How many IVF cycles does your clinic perform each year? Of those, how many are egg donor cycles?

4. What are your donor egg success rates? Are they listed individually or as your clinic as a whole? If listed together, what are your physicians' individual statistics?

5. How many frozen embryos does your typical egg donor cycle produce? What are your freeze–thaw success rates?

6. Does your clinic perform PGD? If so, how many embryos can you expect to end up with?

7. Does your clinic take most embryos to the blastocyst stage, or do you use three-day stage embryos for transfer?

8. Do you have a list of referrals we can contact?

9. Will we have a single point of contact (a nurse coordinator) during our cycle, or is there a team we'll be working with?

10. What board certifications and professional medical memberships do the specialists on your staff hold?

11. What's the average length of tenure for your staff and physicians?

12. What are your clinic's guidelines/preferences for the preferred age for egg donors?

13. Given our medical history, how much importance would you place on using a proven egg donor versus a first-time donor?

14. Does your clinic participate in shared cycles if that's an option we would like to explore?

15. What can we expect as a typical time frame for you or your staff to get back to us if we have questions or concerns?

16. Do you have a list or a preferred egg donation agency that you've worked with in the past?

Appendix B—Interview Questions for Egg Donor Agencies

1. How long have you been in business and/or working in this field?

2. How many donors have your agency matched with recipients in the last year?

3. Do you have references from clinics and previous client/parents?

4. How many donors do you have available in your agency?

5. What is the agency's refund policy?

6. What are your agency's fees and what exactly do they cover?

7. Does your agency provide a service agreement between the egg donor agency and the intended parent?

8. How much is your typical donor compensation, and when/how is that compensation given to the donor?

9. Do you allow your donors to set their own level of compensation?

10. Does your agency require egg donors to undergo psychological screening before being placed on the prospective donor list or after they have been chosen? Who performs the screening (i.e., the agency or a third-party psychological professional)?

11. If we were to desire an open egg donation, will your agency facilitate a meeting between us and the egg donor?

12. Does your agency facilitate anonymous, open, or both kinds of egg donations?

13. How does your egg donor agency manage its information and records regarding its donors?

14. Where does your agency keep this information?

15. How long will the agency keep this information? If for instance the agency goes out of business, who would be responsible for keeping information on past clients, previous cycles, and egg donors in case a need were to arise to contact an egg donor?

16. Does the agency adhere to the American Society for Reproductive Medicine (ASRM) guidelines for egg donation?

17. What kind of medical insurance coverage for the egg donor does your agency provide and what are the terms? Are these costs included in our fees to the agency or paid separately to the insurance company?

18. Who provides the legal contract between the intended parent and the egg donor? Do we need to secure our own reproductive attorney?

19. How are recipient parents protected in the event the egg donor chooses to discontinue the process halfway through a cycle? How is the recipient parent protected in the event the egg donor doesn't take her medication as agreed?

20. Do your agency's fees change depending on our method of payment (e.g., cash, credit card, wire transfer, check)?

21. What are the typical donor fee ranges? What causes one donor's fee to be higher than another's?

22. Does your agency provide an itemized list of expenses?

23. What can we expect regarding contact with the agency during the cycle?

Appendix C—Resources and Questions for the Donor Selection Phase

Questions for Intended Parents to Answer Prior to and During Donor Selection

- What are the most important qualities for my donor (physical, health history, lifestyle, personality, etc.)?
- What is my budget for an egg donor's fees?
- Are there any deal breakers for us on donor characteristics (i.e., eye color, height, etc.)? Convey these to your agency or in-house donor coordinator at your fertility clinic.
- What guidelines does my fertility specialist requests that I follow when selecting a donor (i.e., age, previous or proven donor status, local versus out-of-area, etc.)?

Checklist for Intended Parents Prior to Confirming a Donor Selection

- Has she had a previous donation, and if so, was your doctor's office given all of the medical information needed to make an informed decision on your behalf?
- If you want to meet your donor, did she agree to this? Will you meet before, during, or after the cycle? Was there an agreement to future contact? What was agreed upon (i.e., will the contact go through the agency, clinic, attorney, e-mail, phone number exchange, or third-party donor/sibling registry)?
- Is your donor okay with *you* making the choice on what to do with the remaining embryos (i.e., save them for future siblings, adopt them to another family, donate them to science, etc.)?

- Does your donor have any blackout dates (i.e., unchangeable vacations, school, work or family obligations, etc.) that you need to be aware of that could impact your cycle schedule?

- Did your donor reconfirm that all of the information in her medical history was up-to-date and accurate? Are there any specific questions you have that were not asked on the agency application that you would like answered to help you move forward?

- If she has unusually high SAT/ACT scores or goes to a prestigious college, was your agency able to obtain a copy of her scores or transcripts?

- Do you require a background check? Will your agency help facilitate this?

- Has your donor revealed to her family that she is donating? If not, will she proceed despite any objection should they find out during the course of the cycle?

- If she was a previous donor with your current agency, did they provide you with her genetic and psychological evaluations prior to the signing of your donor agreement and any money exchanging hands?

- If you have chosen a first-time donor and you are not comfortable with the results of her psychological and genetic evaluations, how much of your program fee is refundable (if any)? Is the donor given any portion of her fee?

- If an unmarried donor has a sexual partner, is her partner willing to be tested for communicable diseases? Is her partner supportive? Are they okay with abstaining from sexual activity throughout the injection phase of the process?

- When was her last menstrual period start date? What type of birth control is she on?

- Did you both agree and finalize her fee? Is everything you need in writing with the agency?

Appendix D—Genetic Testing

Genetic Interview Checklist

When your donor has her interview with a licensed geneticist, they'll inquire about the following to build a genetic profile for her and make recommendations for any further lab testing they feel is warranted.

- Donor's pregnancy history
- Donor's health history
- Personal or family history of mental retardation or birth defects
- Personal or family history of stillbirth/miscarriage/neonatal death
- Personal/family history of mental health and substance abuse issues
- Personal/family history of learning disability such as ADD, dyslexia, autism, Asperger's

Standard Lab Tests Your IVF Clinic May Order for Your Donor*

Standard
- Cystic fibrosis
- CBC

Asian, Mediterranean, and African descent
- Hemoglobin electrophoresis as screen for thalassemias and sickle cell trait

Jewish descent
- Multiple tests

---

*Some of these tests have ethnic risk factors and are not required of every population.

Common optional
- Karyotype
- Spinal muscular atrophy
- Fragile X

Advancements in Comprehensive Genetic Testing for Egg Donors
(contributed by Amy Vance, board-certified genetic counselor)

Recently, several laboratories have begun offering genetic tests that screen for more than 100 different (mostly) recessive genes. Population statistics estimate that each person carries between five and eight mutations in genes associated with autosomal recessive genetic disorders. Mutations in DNA typically cause genes not to function properly. However, with autosomal recessive genes, one functional copy is enough to preserve health and thus carriers of recessive gene mutations are expected to be unaffected.

Recessive genes generally do not cause any symptoms or problems. We usually don't know which ones we carry unless a genetic test uncovers them. If two people carry mutations in the same recessive gene, there is a 25% chance that their offspring would inherit each nonworking gene, which could result in a genetic disease. The diseases screened for in the carrier panel vary widely from mild conditions to severe conditions.

Many IVF clinics and/or physicians either require or suggest all egg donors undergo this form of genetic carrier testing. Although the pros may seem to outweigh the cons in our information age, there are some issues that may arise when you test for so many carrier genes. Like the old adage "if you search for something hard enough, you're bound to find something bad." To ensure informed decision making about whether to have your donor take one of these tests, consider the following:

- The purpose of the test
- Test positive rate (20–30%)
- Limitations of the test (such as limitations in detection rates because this is still "new science")
- Possible inability of intended parent to use the donor they have selected because of a positive test result if the IVF center will not use a screen-positive donor

- Potential consequences:
  - Disclosure of the results

    Does a donor have an obligation to inform her insurance company?

    Privacy of the donor to release this information to her intended parents, clinic, and any egg donation agencies she's currently working with or has worked with

    Ethical obligation of the intended parents to pay for genetic counseling for the donor should she be found to be a carrier for a genetic defect (regardless of whether the cycle continues or not)

For many of the conditions tested on these large panels, population carrier frequency is well below 1%. The detection rates (the chance that if you are a carrier, this test will identify your mutation) can be very low as well, sometimes 10% or less.

Appendix E—Medical Team Resources

Genetic Counselor
Amy Vance
(415) 453-4384

Therapists
Abigail Glass, MFT
(818) 903-6399

Brenda Hardt-Fahn, MS, MFT
(310) 994-3817

Carole Lieber Wilkins, MFT
(310) 470-9049

Reproductive Endocrinologists
John Hesla, MD
Oregon Reproductive Medicine
www.oregonreproductivemedicine.com
(503) 274-4994

Bradford Kolb, MD
Huntington Reproductive Center
   Medical Group
www.havingbabies.com
(626) 440-9161

David Tourgeman, MD
Huntington Reproductive Center
   Medical Group
www.havingbabies.com
(818) 788-7288

Daniel Potter, MD
Huntington Reproductive Center
   Medical Group
www.havingbabies.com
(949) 287-5600

Guy Ringler, MD
California Fertility Partners
www.californiafertilitypartners.com
(310) 828-4008

Gregory Rosen, MD
Reproductive Partners Medical
   Group
www.reproductivepartners.com
(877) 273-7763

Vicken Sahakian, MD
Pacific Fertility Center
www.pfcla.com
(310) 209-7700

Eric Scott Sills, MD
Pacific Reproductive Center
www.pacificreproductivecenter.com
(866) 239-2998

Support Group Contributor
Marna Gatlin
Founder, Parents Via Egg
   Donation
www.pved.org
marna@pved.org
(503) 369-9363

*Surrogacy and Egg Donor
   Agency Contributors*

Lilly Frost
www.mydonorcycle.com

Stephanie Goldman-Levich
www.familycreations.net

Kathryn Kaycoff-Manos
www.agency4solutions.com

Elliott Kronenfeld
www.circlesurrogacy.com

Steve Masler
www.thedonorsource.com

Attorneys

Kate Lyon
Lyon Family Formation Law
(310) 745-0216

Steven Lazarus
Lazarus Law Firm
(310) 496-5758

Appendix F—Support Groups and Online Resources for Intended Parents

U.S.-Based Resources

American Society for Reproductive Medicine (ASRM): www.asrm.org
Parents Via Egg Donation (PVED): www.pved.org
RESOLVE: The National Infertility Association: www.resolve.org
Society for Assisted Reproductive Technologies (SART): www.sart.org
The American Surrogacy Center (TASC): www.surrogacy.com

U.K.-Based Resources

National Gamete Donation Trust (NGDT): www.ngdt.co.uk
Donor Conception Network (DCN): www.donor-conception-network.org

Australian Resources

Aussie Egg Donors (AED): www.aussieeggdonors.com
Donor Conception Support Group (DCSG): www.dcsg.org.au

Appendix G—Sample Letters

During the egg donation process, it's not uncommon for letters to change hands between intended parents and donors. We've included two sample letters, one each from an intended parent to a donor and one in return from a donor to her agency, to provide some inspiration in case you feel like writing a letter of your own.

From an Intended Parent to Donor

To my wonderful donor,

I'm the intended parent with whom you've agreed to share a very precious part of yourself. Wendie and Tina of Gifted Journeys have allowed me the opportunity to convey to you my appreciation, and, more generally, my thoughts about this "journey" and myself.

I'm still very close to my family and noticed that you are too. Your biographical notes state that your father is of German descent. So is mine, although he's German/Jewish. Your mother is of Russian/Jewish descent. So is mine. Thus, for starters, you and I share somewhat of a similar ethnic ancestry. Perhaps that's one of the reasons, just one, that I was drawn to you.

I am also a vegetarian, and that means no fish, either. Although I do eat dairy products and egg products. I went meatless about 14 years ago for ethical, aesthetic, and health reasons. I'm an animal lover (do I prefer them over people? hmmmmm).

A friend of mine had twins going through a similar process to myself. Intended parents in the IVF process who need an egg donor usually have access to a large number of potential donors to choose from. But how do you choose? What are you looking for? How do the qualities of the donor translate into qualities in the child? And who would be a good match for me? It's so overwhelming.

But finally, among the hundreds of potential donors, I chose to ask you. You have so many qualities that stand out. You're beautiful, educated, ambitious, athletic, and have a generous spirit. Those are precisely the qualities I hope are passed on to my child.

I asked Wendie about your personality. She told me about how positive and upbeat you are, and that means so much to me. Yes, mental and physical qualities are essential, but I'm nothing if not upbeat. I distance myself from moody and depressed people. Positive attitude is primary to me, and, I believe, a foundation for success in life.

If we're successful with this pregnancy, and a child is created, it shouldn't come as a surprise to you that I will be thinking about you for the rest of my life. A lot. Which leads me to say what I really want to tell you: What you're giving to me is the most important thing anybody could give . . . life itself.

To say "thank you" doesn't come close to expressing my feelings. It would take a Shakespeare or a Tolstoy to come up with the words to articulate what's in my heart, yet I must say, thank you. I plan on being the best father ever. And through these few words, I hope you now know that my gratitude to you for becoming my partner in creating this life will never go away. How could it?

Thank you from the bottom of my heart. . . .

Donor Letter to Her Agency

When I was young, I heard a story about a woman who couldn't have children so her sister became a surrogate for her.

I thought that was the most amazing story and thought someday I wanted to help someone in a life-changing way like that. Years went by and I saw an ad for egg donation. A gay couple was looking for eggs they could use for their surrogate. It made me think of the story from when I was little, and being a human right activist it seemed like an amazing opportunity. I didn't really know anything about egg donation, but it was during the gay marriage debate and I knew I had to get involved. I have been a volunteer for gay rights organizations, but this gave me the chance to literally give a part of myself to the cause.

I started researching information, egg donation agencies, and anything else I needed to know about the egg donation process. When I found your agency, I knew it was a perfect match. The ladies were so warm and informative. I never felt scared of the process or afraid to ask questions along the way. Working with them has enhanced the experience more than I could have ever expected.

I was matched to a couple pretty quickly, and I knew it was meant to be. I have never met any of my couples, but there is still the most amazing bond and love between us. I never knew I could love people so much that I never met! I cannot imagine a better way to help others than to help give them a family. I know what people have to go through sometimes to make a family and if I can be a part of making that easier, and making that dream come true, there is nothing that could keep me from doing so. I am so happy I made the choice to donate because it has been the most amazing experience of my life.

Appendix H—List of States with Favorable Surrogacy Laws

Alabama
Alaska
Arkansas
California
Colorado
Connecticut
Delaware
Florida
Georgia
Hawaii
Idaho
Illinois
Indiana
Iowa
Kansas
Kentucky
Louisiana
Maine
Maryland
Massachusetts
Minnesota
Mississippi
Missouri
Montana
Nebraska

Nevada
New Hampshire
New Jersey
North Carolina
North Dakota
Ohio
Oklahoma
Oregon
Pennsylvania
Rhode Island
South Carolina
South Dakota
Tennessee
Texas
Vermont
Virginia
West Virginia
Wisconsin
Wyoming

Glossary—Insider's Guide to Egg Donation

Abnormality(ies): an abnormal feature, characteristic, or occurrence, typically in amedical context: *a chromosome abnormality.*

AFA (American Fertility Association): a national not-for-profit organization headquartered in New York City. It provides men and women, health care professionals, public officials, and the media—both nationally and internationally—with information about infertility treatments, reproductive and sexual health, and family building options, including adoption and third-party solutions.

Allele: one of two or more alternative forms of a gene that arise by mutation and are found at the same place on a chromosome.

American Society for Reproductive Medicine (ASRM): a multidisciplinary organization dedicated to the advancement of the art, science, and practice of reproductive medicine. The Society accomplishes its mission through the pursuit of excellence in education and research and through advocacy on behalf of patients, physicians, and affiliated health care providers.

Anesthesia: insensitivity to pain, especially as artificially induced by the administration of gases or the injection of drugs before surgical operations. The induction of this state, or the branch of medicine concerned with it.

Antagonist: a substance that interferes with or inhibits the physiological action of another.

Antral Follicle Count: involves counting the resting follicles that are found on the ovary at the beginning of each menstrual cycle, indication of the ovarian reserve of a woman.

Aspiration: the action of drawing fluid by suction from a vessel or cavity.

Assisted Reproductive Technology (ART): is a general term referring to methods used to achieve pregnancy by artificial or partially artificial means. It is reproductive technology used primarily in infertility treatments. The term includes any reproductive technique involving a third party (e.g., a sperm donor, egg donor, or gestational carrier).

Autosomal dominant: one of several ways that a trait or disorder can be passed down through families. If a disease is autosomal dominant, it means you only need to get the abnormal gene from one parent in order for you to inherit the disease. One of the parents may often have the disease.

Baseline Ultrasound: an ultrasound between the first and fifth days of the menstrual cycle, specifically looking to see that there are no cysts.

Blastocyst: a mammalian blastula in which some differentiation of cells has occurred. It possesses an inner cell mass (ICM) or embryoblast, which subsequently forms the embryo, and an outer layer of cells or trophoblast, which later forms the placenta.

Centers for Disease Control and Prevention (CDC): a US Federal Agency under the Department of Health and Human Services. It works to protect public health and safety by providing information to enhance health decisions, and it promotes health through partnerships with state health departments and other organizations. The CDC focus national attention on developing and applying disease prevention and control (especially infectious diseases and foodborne pathogens and other microbial infections), environmental health, occupational safety and health, health promotion, injury prevention, and education activities designed to improve the health of the people of the United States.

Chromosome: an organized structure of DNA and protein found in cells. It is a single piece of coiled DNA containing many genes, regulatory elements, and other nucleotide sequences. Chromosomes also contain DNA-bound proteins, which serve to package the DNA and control its functions.

Compensation: something, typically money, given to someone (i.e., egg donor or surrogate) as a recompense for time, effort, and pain/suffering.

Conception: also known as fertilization, the fusion of gametes to produce a new organism.

Contraception: the deliberate use of artificial methods or other techniques to prevent pregnancy as a consequence of sexual intercourse. The major forms of artificial contraception are: barrier methods, of which the commonest is the condom; the contraceptive pill, which contains synthetic sex hormones that prevent ovulation in the female; intrauterine devices, such as the IUD, which prevent the fertilized ovum from implanting in the uterus; and male or female sterilization.

Counseling: the provision of assistance and guidance in resolving personal, social, or psychological problems and difficulties, especially by a professional.

Cryopreservation: a process where cells or whole tissues are preserved by cooling to low subzero temperatures, such as (typically) 77 K or $-196°C$ (the boiling point of liquid nitrogen). At these low temperatures, any biological activity, including the biochemical reactions that would lead to cell death, is effectively stopped.

Cycle: the period of time taken to complete a single sequence of such events (i.e., the cells are shed over a cycle of 28 days).

Cyst: a membranous sac or cavity of abnormal character containing fluid; a closed sac, having a distinct membrane and division on the nearby tissue. It may contain air, fluids, or semisolid material.

Cystic Fibrosis (CF): a disease passed down through families that causes thick, sticky mucus to build up in the lungs, digestive tract, and other areas of the body. It is one of the most common chronic lung diseases in children and young adults. It is a life-threatening disorder.

Deoxyribonucleic Acid (DNA): a nucleic acid that contains the genetic instructions used in the development and functioning of all known living organisms. The DNA segments that carry this genetic information are called genes, but other DNA sequences have structural purposes or are involved in regulating the use of this genetic information.

Dominant: genetics relating to or denoting heritable characteristics that are controlled by genes that are expressed in offspring even when inherited from only one parent. Often contrasted with **recessive**.

Egg donation: the process by which a woman provides one or several (usually 10–15) eggs (ova, oocytes) for purposes of assisted reproduction or biomedical research. For assisted reproduction purposes, egg donation involves the process of in vitro fertilization as the eggs are fertilized in the laboratory. After the eggs have been obtained, the role of the *egg donor* is complete. Egg donation is part of the process of third party reproduction as part of ART.

Embryo: an unborn human baby, especially in the first eight weeks from conception, after implantation but before all the organs are developed.

Estradiol (E2): is the most potent estrogen of a group of endogenous estrogen steroids. In women, estradiol is responsible for growth of the breast and reproductive epithelia, maturation of long bones, and development of the secondary sexual characteristics. Estradiol is produced mainly by the ovaries with secondary production by the adrenal glands and conversion of steroid precursors into estrogens in fat tissue. During the early part of the menstrual cycle, estradiol levels remain nearly constant. This is followed by a rapid increase reaching a peak the day before or the day of ovulation. It is generally believed that the rise in estradiol is the factor which triggers LH release. Following ovulation, there is a drop in estradiol followed by a second rise. At menopause, estrogen concentrations in the body fall to low levels. This decrease is often accompanied by vascular instability (hot flashes and night sweats), a rise in incidence of heart disease, and an increasing rate of bone loss (osteoporosis). Estradiol levels are used to assess fertility, amenorrhea, and precocious puberty in girls.

Estrogen: any of a group of steroid hormones that promote the development and maintenance of female characteristics of the body. Such hormones are also produced artificially for use in oral contraceptives or to treat menopausal and menstrual disorders.

Ethics: the discipline dealing with what is good and bad and with moral duty and obligation.

Fibroid: a benign tumor of muscular and fibrous tissues, typically developing in the wall of the uterus.

Follicles: (ovarian) follicles are the basic units of female reproductive biology, each of which is composed of roughly spherical aggregations of cells found in the ovary. They contain a single oocyte (immature ovum or egg). These structures are periodically initiated to grow and develop, culminating in ovulation of usually a single competent oocyte in humans. These eggs/ova are only developed once every menstrual cycle.

Follistim (follitropin beta injection): approved for women to help healthy ovaries to develop and release mature eggs. Follistim is also for women participating in an ART program to help the ovaries produce more mature eggs. Follistim is also approved for men to help bring about the production and development of sperm.

Fragile-X: a genetic syndrome that is the most commonly known single-gene cause of autism and the most common inherited cause of intellectual disability. It results in a spectrum of characteristic physical and intellectual limitations and emotional and behavioral features which range from severe to mild in manifestation.

Frozen Embryo Transfer (FET): a procedure which takes embryos that have been frozen for a period of time and replaces them in the uterus after they have been thawed. FET is a relatively non-invasive procedure, which is why many couples choose to have it performed. It can be successfully performed on women who are experiencing either natural or controlled menstrual cycles.

Gamete: a mature haploid male or female germ cell that is able to unite with another of the opposite sex in sexual reproduction to form a zygote.

Genetic Testing: screening which allows the genetic diagnosis of vulnerabilities to inherited diseases and can also be used to determine a child's paternity (genetic father) or a person's ancestry. Because genetic testing may open up ethical or psychological problems, genetic testing is often accompanied by genetic counseling.

Genotype: the genetic makeup of an organism or group of organisms with reference to a single trait, set of traits, or an entire complex of traits.

Gestational Carrier (Surrogate): a woman who carries and delivers a child for another couple or person. This woman may carry the pregnancy to delivery after having an embryo to which she has no genetic relationship whatsoever, transferred to her uterus (called gestational surrogacy), or she may be the child's genetic mother (called traditional surrogacy). If the pregnant woman received compensation for carrying and delivering the child (besides medical and other reasonable expenses) the arrangement is called a commercial surrogacy, otherwise the arrangement is sometimes referred to as an altruistic surrogacy.

Gonadotropin (glycoprotein hormone): a protein hormone secreted by gonadotrope cells of the pituitary glands of vertebrates. These hormones are central to the complex endocrine system that regulates normal growth, sexual development, and reproductive function. The hormones LH and FSH are secreted by the anterior pituitary gland, whereas hCG and eCG are secreted by the placenta.

HCG (human chorionic gonadotropin): a hormone produced in the human placenta that maintains the corpus luteum during pregnancy.

HIPAA (Health Insurance Portability and Accountability Act): a 1996 Federal law that restricts access to individuals' private medical information.

Hormone: a regulatory substance produced in an organism and transported in tissue fluids such as blood or sap to stimulate specific cells or tissues into action.

Implantation: the attachment of the fertilized egg or blastocyst to the wall of the uterus at the start of pregnancy, often delayed in some mammals by several months.

Infertility: primarily refers to the biological inability of a person to contribute to conception. Infertility may also refer to the state of a woman who is unable to carry a pregnancy to full term. There are many biological causes of infertility, some which may be bypassed with medical intervention.

Injection (or "shot"): is an infusion method of putting fluid into the body, usually with a hollow needle and a syringe which is pierced through the skin to a sufficient depth for the material to be forced into the body. There are several methods of injection, including subcutaneous, intramuscular, and intravenous.

Intracytoplasmic Sperm Injection (ICSI): a technique developed to help achieve fertilization for couples with severe male factor infertility or couples who have had failure to fertilize in a previous in vitro fertilization attempt. The procedure overcomes many of the barriers to fertilization and allows couples with little hope of achieving successful pregnancy to obtain fertilized embryos. The technique involves very precise maneuvers to pick up a single live sperm and inject it directly into the center of a human egg. The embryologist picks up the single live sperm in a glass needle and injects it directly into the egg.

Intramuscular: situated or taking place within, or administered into a muscle (i.e., intramuscular injection).

In Vitro Fertilization (IVF): (in vitro meaning "in glass") the process of fertilizing an egg is done in a laboratory (in glass tubes) to give couples a better chance at conceiving a child. This type of treatment is generally only undertaken after numerous other therapies have been tried but failed to produce a child.

Karyotype (test): a test to identify and evaluate the size, shape, and number of chromosomes in a sample of body cells. A karyotype is an organized profile of a person's chromosomes, arranged and numbered by size—from largest to smallest. This arrangement helps scientists quickly identify chromosomal alterations that may result in a genetic disorder.

Lupron (leuprolide acetate): injectable medication which indirectly down regulates the secretion of gonadotropins, luteinizing hormone (LH), and follicle-stimulating hormone (FSH) leading to a dramatic reduction in estradiol and testosterone levels in both sexes.

Luteal Phase (Secretory Phase): the latter phase of the menstrual cycle, beginning with the formation of the corpus luteum and ending in either pregnancy or luteolysis. The main hormone associated with this stage is progesterone, which is significantly higher during the luteal phase than other phases of the cycle.

Luteinizing Hormone (LH): helps regulate the menstrual cycle and egg production (ovulation). The level of LH in a woman's body varies with the phase of the menstrual cycle. It increases rapidly just before ovulation occurs, about midway through the cycle (Day 14 of a 28-day cycle). This is called an LH surge. Luteinizing hormone and follicle-stimulating hormone levels rise and fall together during the monthly menstrual cycle. In men, LH stimulates the production of testosterone, which plays a role in sperm production.

Menopause: the period in a woman's life (typically between 45 and 50 years of age) when menstruation ceases.

Menopur: a highly purified preparation of naturally derived gonadotropins called hMG, containing equal amounts (75 IUs) of two kinds of hormonal activity: FSH, which helps stimulate egg production; and LH, which helps the eggs mature and release (ovulate). It helps stimulate eggs to mature in women whose ovaries are basically healthy but are unable to develop eggs. It is usually used together with human chorionic gonadotropin (hCG) and is indicated for the development of multiple follicles and pregnancy in women participating in an ART program.

Miscarriage: the spontaneous loss of a fetus before the 20th week of pregnancy; may also be called a "spontaneous abortion."

Mitosis: a type of cell division that results in two daughter cells each having the same number and kind of chromosomes as the parent nucleus, typical of ordinary tissue growth.

Motility (sperm): a biological term which refers to the ability to move spontaneously and actively, consuming energy in the process. **Sperm motility** describes the ability of sperm to move properly toward an egg, or the "quality" of the sperm, which is a factor in successful pregnancies, as opposed to the "quantity." Sperm that do not properly "swim" will not reach the egg to fertilize it.

Mutation: the changing of the structure of a gene, resulting in a variant form that may be transmitted to subsequent generations, caused by the alteration of single base units in DNA or the deletion, insertion, or rearrangement of larger sections of genes or chromosomes.

National Institutes of Health (NIH): provides leadership and direction to programs designed to improve the health of the nation by conducting and supporting research in the causes, diagnosis, prevention, and cure of human diseases; the processes of human growth and development; the biological effects of environmental contaminants; the understanding of mental, addictive, and physical disorders; and in directing programs for the collection, dissemination, and exchange of information in medicine and health, including the development and support of medical libraries and the training of medical librarians and other health information specialists.

Oocyte: an immature female sex cell.

Ovarian Hyperstimulation Syndrome (OHSS): a condition occurring as a result of taking hormonal medications that stimulate the development of eggs in a woman's ovaries, which become swollen and painful. About one-fourth of women who take injectable fertility drugs get a mild form of OHSS, which goes away after about a week. A small proportion of women taking fertility drugs develop a more severe form, which can cause rapid weight gain, abdominal pain, vomiting and shortness of breath, and can last for weeks.

Ovulation: the process in a female's menstrual cycle by which a mature ovarian follicle ruptures and discharges an ovum (also known as an oocyte, female gamete, or egg).

Pituitary: the major endocrine gland; a pea-sized body attached to the base of the brain. The pituitary is important in controlling growth and development and the functioning of the other endocrine glands.

Polycystic Ovarian Syndrome (PCOS): a condition in which there is an imbalance of a woman's female sex hormones. Too much androgen hormone is made, along with changes in other hormone levels. This hormone imbalance may cause changes in the menstrual cycle, skin changes, small cysts in the ovaries, trouble getting pregnant, and other problems.

Preimplantation Genetic Diagnosis (PGD): also known as embryo screening, a procedure performed on embryos prior to implantation, sometimes even on oocytes prior to fertilization. PGD is considered another way to prenatal diagnosis and requires IVF to obtain oocytes or embryos for evaluation.

Premature Ovarian Failure: a loss of normal function of the ovaries before the age of 40. If ovaries fail, they don't produce normal amounts of the hormone estrogen or release eggs regularly. Infertility is a common result. Women with premature ovarian failure—also known as primary ovarian insufficiency—may have irregular or occasional periods for years and may even become pregnant.

Progesterone: a steroid hormone released by the corpus luteum that stimulates the uterus to prepare for pregnancy.

Psychological Screening (Evaluation or Assessment): The assessment includes social and biographical information, direct observations, and data from specific psychological tests. Psychological assessment may involve the use of tools such as questionnaires, checklists and rating scales, and/or an interview. The psychologist or related licensed professional will sometimes start by asking questions of the person being evaluated, but not always. In psychological evaluations, the administration of standardized psychological tests (i.e., MMPI, NEO-PI) either by a psychologist or by someone the psychologist supervises is often a component of the evaluation.

Recessive: genetics relating to or denoting heritable characteristics controlled by genes that are expressed in offspring only when inherited from both parents; that is, when not masked by a dominant characteristic inherited from one parent; often contrasted with "dominant."

Reproduction (or procreation): the biological process by which new "offspring" individual organisms are produced from their "parents." Sexual reproduction typically requires the involvement of two individuals or gametes, one each from the opposite type of sex.

Reproductive Endocrinology (RE): a surgical subspecialty of obstetrics and gynecology that trains physicians in reproductive medicine addressing hormonal functioning as it pertains to reproduction as well as the issue of infertility. Although most RE specialists primarily focus on the treatment of infertility, reproductive endocrinologists are trained to also evaluate and treat hormonal dysfunctions in females and males outside of infertility. Reproductive endocrinologists have specialty training in obstetrics and gynecology (OB/GYN) before they undergo subspecialty training (fellowship) in RE.

Retrieval (Egg): also called "aspiration," it is performed 36 hours after hCG injection. Sedation by an anesthesiologist is administered through an intravenous catheter (a small tube in an arm vein). The patient is not completely asleep but in a sort of twilight state, remembering very little of the retrieval. After sedation, the vagina is washed with a salt water solution. A needle is placed under ultrasound guidance into the ovary and fluid and eggs from the follicles in the ovaries are collected into a test tube and sent to the IVF lab. The whole procedure takes about 30 minutes, and discomfort is generally minimal. On average, eggs will be retrieved from over two-thirds of the follicles.

Secondary Infertility: the inability to become pregnant or to carry a pregnancy to term, following the birth of one or more biological children. The birth of the first child does not involve any assisted reproductive technologies or fertility medications.

Sexually Transmitted Disease (STD): an illness that has a significant probability of transmission between humans by means of sexual behavior or activity, including sexual intercourse.

Sickle Cell Anemia: Sickle cell anemia is a disease passed down through families in which red blood cells form an abnormal crescent shape. It is much more common in people of African and Mediterranean descent. It is also seen in people from South and Central America, the Caribbean, and the Middle East.

Stimulate: raise levels of physiological or nervous activity in the body or any biological system, that is, women are given fertility drugs to stimulate their ovaries.

Stimulation Medications ("stims" or "meds"): commonly used with IUI and IVF to treat ovulation disorders and unexplained infertility. They stimulate the growth and development of ovarian follicles to produce multiple eggs and increase the chance of pregnancy. Depending on the medication, it may be in pill form or injectable.

Subcutaneous (injection): administered under the skin.

Surrogacy: an arrangement for a woman to carry and give birth to a child who will be raised by others.

Technology: the making, usage and knowledge of tools, techniques, systems, or methods of organization to solve a problem or serve some purpose. The term can either be applied generally or to specific areas, such as *medical or reproductive technology.*

Test Tube: also known as a culture tube or sample tube; a thin glass tube closed at one end used to hold small amounts of material for laboratory testing or experiments.

Transfer (Embryo): a step in the process of assisted reproduction in which one or several embryos are placed into the uterus of a female with the intent to establish a pregnancy. This technique is often used in connection with IVF.

Transvaginal Ultrasound: a type of pelvic ultrasound used to look at a woman's reproductive organs, including the uterus, ovaries, cervix, and vagina. Transvaginal means across or through the vagina.

Uterine Lining: also termed the "endometrium," it is the inner membrane of the uterus. During the menstrual cycle, the endometrium grows to a thick, blood vessel-rich, glandular tissue layer. This represents an optimal environment for the implantation of a blastocyst upon its arrival in the uterus.

The endometrium detectable using ultrasound scanners and has an average thickness of 6.7 mm.

Vitrification: a specialized freezing technique, which freezes the egg so quickly ice crystals don't have time to form.

Zygote (a fertilized ovum): the initial cell formed when two gamete cells are joined by means of sexual reproduction. It is the earliest developmental stage of the embryo. A zygote is always synthesized from the union of two gametes and constitutes the first stage in a unique organism's development. Zygotes are usually produced by a fertilization event between two haploid cells—an ovum from a female and a sperm cell from a male—which combine to form the single diploid cell. Such zygotes contain DNA derived from both the mother and the father, and this provides all the genetic information necessary to form a new individual.

References

Chapter 1

1. Centers for Disease Control and Prevention, American Society for Reproductive Medicine, and Society for Assisted Reproductive Technology. 2010. *2008 Assisted Reproductive Technology Success Rates: National Summary and Fertility Clinic Reports*. Atlanta, GA: U.S. Department of Health and Human Services.
2. Centers for Disease Control and Prevention. 2010. *2008 Assisted Reproductive Technology Success Rates: National Summary and Fertility Clinic Reports. Section 1: Overview*. Atlanta, GA: U.S. Department of Health and Human Services.
3. Human Fertilisation and Embryology Authority. 2010. *Fertility Facts and Figures 2008*. London: Human Fertilisation and Embryology Authority.
4. Centers for Disease Control and Prevention. 2010. *2008 Assisted Reproductive Technology Success Rates: National Summary and Fertility Clinic Reports. Section 4: ART Cycles Using Donor Eggs*. Atlanta, GA: U.S. Department of Health and Human Services.
5. Kurinczuk, Jennifer J., and Chris Hockley. 2010. *Fertility Treatment in 2006: A Statistical Analysis*, 173. London: Human Fertilisation and Embryology Authority.
6. Human Fertilisation and Embryology Authority. 2010. *Fertility Facts and Figures 2008*, 6. London: Human Fertilisation and Embryology Authority.

Chapter 3

7. Ethics Committee of the American Society for Reproductive Medicine. 2007. "Financial Compensation of Oocyte Donors." *Fertility and Sterility* 88 (2): 305–9.

Chapter 4

8. Centers for Disease Control and Prevention, American Society for Reproductive Medicine, and Society for Assisted Reproductive Technology. 2011. *2009 Assisted Reproductive Technology Success Rates: National Summary and Fertility Clinic Reports.* Atlanta, GA: U.S. Department of Health and Human Services.

9. Staessen, Catherine, Peter Platteau, Elvire Van Assche, An Michiels, Herman Tournaye, Michel Camus, Paul Devroey, Inge Liebaers, and André Van Steirteghem. 2004. "Comparison of Blastocyst Transfer with or without Preimplantation Genetic Diagnosis for Aneuploidy Screening in Couples with Advanced Maternal Age: A Prospective Randomized Controlled Trial." *Human Reproduction* 19 (12): 2849–58.

Chapter 7

10. Sunkara, Sesh Kamal, Vivian Rittenberg, Nick Raine-Fening, Siladitya Bhattacharya, Javier Zamora, and Arri Coomarasamy. 2011. "Association between the Number of Eggs and Live Birth in IVF Treatment: An Analysis of 400 135 Treatment Cycles." *Oxford Journals.*

11. Sunkara, Sesh Kamal, Vivian Rittenberg, Nick Raine-Fenning, Siladitya Bhattacharya, Javier Zamora, and Arri Coomarasamy. 2011. "Association between the Number of Eggs and Live Birth in IVF Treatment: An Analysis of 400 135 Treatment Cycles." *Human Reproduction* 26 (7): 1768–74.

Index